Praise for
Mrs. B's Guide to Household Witchery

"Kris Bradley does amazing things to bring the spirit of the witch to everyday life, both in her blog *Confessions of a Pagan Soccer Mom*  *de to Household Witchery*. She manages to combine the sen ssings of fun, magic, and spirituality. Even if you are no wise, you can find valuable tips, tricks, and ideas to bring

—Christopher Penczak, author, teacher of Witchcraft

"Home is where the magic is! Kris Bradley reminds us to make our home places sacred with her charming ideas for ritualizing daily life. From kitchen to bedroom, here are ideas for every room, every day."

—Patricia Monaghan, author of *Magical Gardens: Cultivating Soil and Spirit*

"Witchcraft is the magic of the hearth, house, family, and community so real witchcraft begins in the home! *Mrs. B's Guide to Household Witchery* will help you to unlock the magic that dwells within each of us and teach you how to apply that magic in your home every day. Let Mrs. B show you how to bless and cleanse every room to protect your household from negativity and harm, whether it be doors and windows or even drain pipes. Discover how to add a little real charm to your home, be it prosperity, love, or harmony. Learn to connect with traditional household deities that can guard over your home and aid you in your magic. This delicious tome is filled with recipes and rituals to make your household a place of pure enchantment!"

—Christian Day, author of *The Witches' Book of the Dead* and owner of Witch shops HEX and OMEN in Salem, and HEX in New Orleans

"There are so many things I like about *Mrs. B's Guide to Household Witchery*. Kris Bradley's writing style is extremely readable but her coverage of the subject is exceptional. I'm especially pleased to see that she makes a point of including the domestic deities, so often ignored by other writers on popular magic. She has a most valuable appendix on gods and goddesses, along with another useful one on herbs and oils. I applaud her inclusion of mention of a child's own Book of Shadows, something so many parents will appreciate. This is a beautifully designed book that I thoroughly and happily recommend."

—Raymond Buckland, author of *Buckland's Book of Gypsy Magic*

Mrs. B's Guide to
HOUSEHOLD WITCHERY

Everyday Magic, Spells, and Recipes

KRIS BRADLEY

WEISERBOOKS
San Francisco, CA / Newburyport, MA

First published in 2012 by Weiser Books
Red Wheel/Weiser, LLC
with offices at:
665 Third Street, Suite 400
San Francisco, CA 94107
www.redwheelweiser.com

ISBN: 978-1-57863-515-3
Library of Congress Cataloging-in-Publication Data available upon request

Cover design by Jim Warner
Interior by Kathryn Sky-Peck

Printed in the United States of America
MAL
10 9 8 7 6 5 4 3 2 1
The paper used in this publication meets the minimum requirements
of the American National Standard for Information Sciences—
Permanence of Paper for Printed Library Materials Z39.48-1992 (R1997).

To my lobster, Bill. There just aren't enough words.
To my family, for their unwavering support and acceptance.
And to the amazing women of the Broom & Brew.
Skyclad vengeance shall be ours!!!

Not only is the universe stranger than we imagine,
it is stranger than we can imagine.
—SIR ARTHUR EDDINGTON

Contents

Acknowledgments

This book would not have been possible without the support and assistance of a multitude of people. Many thanks and much love to my husband and children who picked up slack and ate a lot of sandwiches while this book was being written. A huge thank-you to my parents for a childhood lost in books, sitting in trees, and open to a million possibilities. Thanks to my sister for buying me my first tarot deck when I was twelve, and to my brother who was more of an inspiration than he probably realizes. Much love to all of the members of the Monmouth County Broom & Brew. You ladies make me laugh, keep me sane(ish), and I am so blessed to have you in my life—you've earned your monkey wings, one and all!

I would never have been in the position to write this book if it weren't for everyone who reads *Confessions of a Pagan Soccer Mom*. Thanks for sharing all my mutterings and ramblings. And a special thanks to Nydia Macedo, the very first person to read and comment to the blog! If it hadn't been for you, I might have stopped there.

And thanks to the wonderful people at Weiser Books for holding the hand of a blogger writing her very first book. Your work, help, and tips were more than I could have hoped for.

Introduction

When I started on my path as a Pagan, I read book after book after book. With no Internet and no idea where to even think of finding another Pagan or group to learn with, putting information together for myself was the only thing I had back then. I was strongly drawn to anything based on the domestic part of magic and deity: gods and goddesses of the hearth, kitchen witchery, recipes of all sorts. Over the years, I worked out a system that allowed me to include magic in my everyday life as a wife and stay-at-home mom. With three kids, a houseful of pets, and not a lot of money, these methods had to include things that were already in my home and that could be done in a short amount of time. I came to consider this collection of methods "domestic witchery," and I eventually started a blog called *Confessions of a Pagan Soccer Mom*, where I shared my ideas and thoughts on the subject.

This book contains the basics of it all, though I do not consider it a "101" book. While I hope it will help point the way to beginners who are interested in taking a domestic path, it's based on the idea that readers have a general knowledge of magical practice and Pagan religious traditions already. This book won't teach you how to be a Pagan, but it will hopefully lead you to some ideas on creating a house filled with magic and give you a broader view of what it means to be domestic. And though it mentions the holidays that I personally take part in, I believe that many of the ideas in this book can be incorporated into any spiritual practice. I hope you enjoy!

WHAT IS A DOMESTIC WITCH?

Domestic witchery is a magical practice based on bringing magic and deity into the mundane of everyday domestic life. It's the realization that even the simplest household chores can be transformed to influence the energies in our home and lives; every chore can honor our families, deity, and ourselves.

Does that mean working like a slave to carry out the every whim of our families? Or turning into the stereotypical 1950s housewife with a pristine house, dishpan hands, and a smile plastered on her face (not to mention a flask tucked into her apron)? Not at all. Many domestic witches *do* set their sights on being similar to that fifties mom in the sense of being available to their children, taking pride in their home, and cooking family meals. They are attempting to restore things that have started to get put on the back burner in this busy, often chaotic world. However, being a domestic witch is still about being a modern witch who works as an equal to their partner and with their chosen deity to make a warm, welcoming environment in their home. For those who choose to be parents, it's also about bringing up healthy, happy children who are self-sufficient, self-assured, and who have a well-rounded spiritual upbringing.

Can a man be a domestic witch? Sure! Any man who wants to create a home that is a haven can work with magic to create the place he craves. Whether single or in a partnership, there is no reason why today's modern male can't take on the role of creating a magical household. Male domestic witches take pride in their homes, their land, their families. Domestic witchery is all about a love of caring for their hearth, home, family, and the deities who oversee them—not about gender!

In this book we'll explore deities that traditionally watch over the home, find out ways to use your ceiling fan as a tool of the element of Air, learn to mix up a prosperity oil straight from your kitchen cabinet, and much more!

one

Making the Mundane Magical Room by Room

One of the first steps on the path of domestic witchery is the simple act of looking at your home in a new way. Instead of seeing heaps of dirty clothes, pots to be scrubbed, and socks to be sorted as chores, view them as opportunities instead. These tasks and others are opportunities to follow a more positive path—openings to interact with deity, to teach your children, and to create magic with almost everything you touch. In this chapter, we're going on a room-by-room tour of the home to explore the potential magic that can spring up in every corner! Each section will include a bit on how to use everyday items to create or enhance magic, as well as a list of those areas of magic that are best for that room and a spell or two. There are also suggestions for creating a family book of shadows (or book of magical information) specifically for some rooms.

Let's start right at your stoop.

DOORWAYS AND THRESHOLDS

A threshold is something sacred.

—PORPHYRY, ANCIENT GREEK PHILOSOPHER

Doorways and thresholds are not just a way for people to enter and leave a house; they are also an opening for energy and spirits, both positive and negative. By creating and maintaining magical thresholds, the domestic witch can construct barriers against those things that you'd rather keep away from your family. The first thing to do to get your thresholds ready is a good herbal cleansing. A magical wash like the Protection Wash in chapter 4 will do the trick. Wipe down the inside and outside of every passage from the outside into your home, including windowsills, doors, and door frames, your dryer vent, attic and crawl space entrances, and garage doors. To clean the actual glass in windows and doors, use a mix of four cups water, one cup vinegar, and one teaspoon of Castile soap or liquid dish detergent in a clean spray bottle. If you have a porch, walkway, or a tile entry to your home, use a clean bucket of cleansing mix to scrub this down as well. An easy way to clean your porch is to

pour a bit of the wash out, use your broom to scrub it in, and sweep the mix away from your door. If you live in an apartment that has carpeting outside your door, consider using a floor sweep on the area right out in front, and then vacuum well.

Once everything is cleansed, it's time to lay down some protective magic outside of your doorway. Find a sturdy broom that you can leave by your door. A broom not only offers its own protective magic, but it can also be used to sweep off your entryway on a regular basis. There are forms of magical practice that include leaving or pouring baneful ingredients on the doorway of a perceived enemy's home, so being in the practice of sweeping off your porch isn't a bad habit to get into!

If you don't have a mat at your front door, now is the time to put one out. Get in the habit of wiping your shoes off before you enter the house; this keeps you from dragging in dirt as well as any maleficent energies that might be clinging to you. On the underside of the mat, use permanent markers or paint pens to draw protective runes, sigils, or even just the word "protection" itself.

There are many ways to add protection to the inside of your doorway as well. A simple and traditional option is to hang a horseshoe over the door, with the opening pointed upward to catch luck and hold it. Iron wards off all manner of unfriendly entities; that's one of the reasons horseshoes are considered lucky. If you don't have a horseshoe on hand, hammering a small iron nail into your door frame can do the trick just as well. Hanging a pair of scissors over or by your door (positioned so that they remain open) is supposed to cut off negativity before it can come inside. In feng shui, adding a mirror to your doorway, facing outside, can help deflect strong negative energies.

You might want to bury a witch bottle right outside your doorway. Witch bottles became popular for repelling evil attacks and magic spells in the sixteenth and seventeenth centuries. Modern witches create them to divert negative energy away from their homes. Recipes for witch bottles vary greatly, but the majority seem to include something sharp (pins, nails, shards of glass) to "impale" the evil that enters the bottle, a liquid (urine, vinegar, wine) to "drown" the evil, and rosemary for protection. Witch bottle recipes might also include such things as hair or nail clippings, feathers, coins, or salt. While some instructions call for the bottle to be buried in the farthest reaches of your property, most say it should be placed right outside your doorway. If you don't have a convenient place to bury your bottle, keep it in the attic, the basement, or in an out-of-the-way spot in the center of your home.

Creating a spell bag to hang near the door can also protect your home and family and bring luck to your door. You can craft a spell bag with a scrap of cloth tied with a ribbon or a store-bought drawstring bag, filled with protective herbs and charms. Unlike a witch bottle, which should remain sealed and left alone, a spell bag can be taken down and added to whenever you wish.

Domestic Witch Bottle

While there are literally dozens and dozens of instructions out there on making a witch bottle, I've planned this one specifically for those who not only want to protect their home, but also want to connect to it in a magical way. If at some point you find you need to replace the broom from which you've taken the tines for this bottle, retire it to the attic or basement, but don't throw it away. Doing so could damage the connection between the bottle and your home.

Items Needed:

- A small jar with a lid or a bottle with a tight-fitting cork
- 1/3 cup salt
- 3 sewing needles or straight pins
- 6 iron nails, the largest that will fit in your jar
- 9 tines from your household broom
- 3 tablespoons of a protection herb (or 1 tablespoon of 3 different herbs), preferably from your own garden (Possible options include star anise, basil, bay leaf, and black pepper.)
- A pinch of dirt from your yard
- Red wine, vinegar, or your own urine to fill the bottle

1. Pour the salt into the jar and say,

   Salt for purification.

2. Add the sewing needles, saying,

   As I myself sew the threads of my family life, may these needles sew safety around me and mine.

3. Place the nails into the jar and say,

   As the nails in our home pierce the wood to hold our home strong, may these nails pierce all negativity and hold it safely away from us.

4. Place the broom straw into the jar and repeat,

   As the broom in my home sweeps away dirt, so may these straws sweep negativity away from this home and its inhabitants.

5. Add the herb(s) and say,

   (Name of herb) strengthens this protection charm.

6. With the addition of the dirt from your yard say:

   This soil binds this jar to my home and property.

5. Pour in the liquid until the jar is almost completely filled, and it's covered all of your ingredients. Hold the jar, concentrating on your feelings of protection toward your family, pets, and property, and say,

Let this wine (vinegar/urine) drown all evil that would seek to touch me and mine.

7. Cap the lid tightly. At this point you can seal the bottle with candle wax if you choose. Add symbols of protection, your family seal, or anything you feel compelled to draw on the lid or the jar itself. When you're finished, take another few minutes to sit quietly and add your intentions to the jar, then bury it as close as you can to your front door.

Front Door Luck and Protection Bag

A luck and protection bag can be created to hang on the inside of your door. You can make one just for the front door, or you can craft one for each door that leads to the outside. Don't forget the garage door! This spell works best at the time of the waxing or full moon.

Items Needed:

- A heatproof dish and a lit self-lighting charcoal disk
- Protection Mix to burn as incense (see chapter 4)
- A white candle
- A lighter or matches
- A silver coin for luck
- A small dish of salt
- A small dish of water
- A small drawstring bag in the color that represents protection or luck to you (red is a good choice for this)
- A sprig of rosemary for protection
- A strip of dried orange rind for happiness
- A tag lock (snippet of hair or nail clippings) from each member of the family, including pets

1. Gather all your spell ingredients. If your magical tradition includes casting a circle, do so now. Add some of the Protection incense to the charcoal to burn, and light the candle.

2. Take the coin in hand and pass it through the smoke of the incense and say,

May this tool of luck be blessed by Air.

3. Pass it over the flame of the candle, saying,

    May this tool of luck be blessed by Fire.

4. Sprinkle a bit of salt onto the coin and say,

    May this tool of luck be blessed by Earth.

5. Finish with a sprinkle of water while saying,

    May this tool of luck be blessed by Water.

6. Place the coin into your drawstring bag.

7. Repeat each action for the rosemary as a tool of protection and the orange rind as a tool of happiness.

8. When your items have all been blessed by the elements, take the tag locks for your family, and add them to the bag one at a time. With each addition repeat,

    For (insert family member or pet's name here), luck, protection, and happiness.

9. Close the bag up tightly with three knots. Hold it in your hands for a few minutes, concentrating on your intentions for luck and protection for your family, and then hang the bag up over or near your door, preferably with a small iron nail.

◆ ◆ ◆

As for windows in your home, a good sprinkling of salt or black salt across the sill works wonders. Pressing two straight pins, slanted toward each other to form an "X" in each corner will give a boost to the window's protective energies. When it's time to wipe down the windows with your vinegar mix, make sure to clean in a clockwise circular motion. When the window is clean, use the cloth or paper towel you cleaned it with to trace a protection symbol over the entire length of the window.

Once your front doorway is cleansed and set up, you may want to mix up a blend of protection herbs in a jar to keep by your door. A combination of dill, flaxseed, garlic, salt, and sage will help protect family members from negativity of all sorts. Each time you give the porch a good sweeping, or when you feel your home could use a little extra protection, sprinkle a handful of the herbs across the threshold to reinforce your boundaries.

Deities Associated with Doorways and Thresholds

Cardea, Hecate, Hermes, Janus, Lima, Mercury, Trivia

THE LIVING ROOM

The happiest moments of my life
have been the few which I have passed
at home in the bosom of my family.
—THOMAS JEFFERSON

The living room should be an area where the whole family can come together. Whether everyone is engaged as a group over a board game, challenging each other for the top score at virtual bowling, or sitting quietly each with a good book, this room should be a place where everyone knows they can come and feel the love of the family.

One of the easiest ways to bring magic and clarity into your life is to make and maintain a living space that is physically and metaphysically uncluttered. Take the time to at least organize or to even clear out what's lying around the room. Get into the habit of doing a major cleaning and cleansing each season. Between these times do what you can to keep things from piling up. A clutter-free home allows more positive energy to flow and increases the success of magical works.

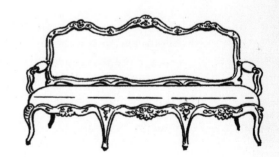

A handy addition to any living room or family room altar is a hearthstone. Not many homes these days require a functioning fireplace, once considered the heart of the home as a source of heat and the main cooking area. You can recreate that magical nexus by finding a flat stone or using a natural stone tile.

Clear off a space on a shelf or set up a small table, and add your stone. Place a large pillar candle on it to be your "hearth fire." A red candle is very appropriate for this; however, a white candle can always fill in. Whenever the family is all together, whether for a simple evening of playing games or for a sabbat celebration, light the hearth candle to add magical vibrations to the gathering. Always light this candle first and use it to light all other candles in your home. When it's burned down and needs replaced, make sure to light the new candle from the old one. Lighting your candles in this way helps establish a tradition of keeping a sacred flame of your home, similar to how hearth fires were once ritually lit for the goddess Hestia.

Hearthstone and Candle Blessing

A fireplace is not something most homes have these days. However, creating your own area to represent the hearth in your home isn't difficult, nor does it need to take up much space. Designating an area to be the hearth of the home creates an instant space for magic, ritual, and honoring the sacred.

Items Needed:

- A large unscented candle
- A carving tool, such as a wooden cooking skewer
- A large flat stone or natural stone tile to represent your hearth
- A lighter or matches

1. Allow everyone in the family to carve into the candle their name, initials, or a symbol that represents them. If you like, add words or symbols to identify things you'd like to encourage in your home, such as peace, joy, protection, or good health.

2. Take the stone and place it in its new, permanent position in your living room. Make sure that it's in a place that can safely hold a lit candle and removed from the reach of pets and small children. Have everyone place the fingers of one hand on the stone and say,

We ask for the blessings of the Lord and Lady on this, the stone that is the heart of our home. This room is where we gather in love, in joy, in sadness, and in celebration.

3. Place the candle on the stone, saying,

    We ask for the blessings of the Lord and Lady on this candle and ask that it burn brightly, always leading us back to the safety and comfort of our home and hearth. So mote it be.

4. Light the candle and allow it to burn as long as you can.

◆ ◆ ◆

A Family Altar

Once you have your hearth set up, you can use it as the base for a family altar. Just add to the area a family photo or an item or picture to represent each member of the household—including pets. Take a few minutes every morning before the family leaves the house to light your hearth candle and say a few quick words to your chosen deity, asking for him or her to watch over your family as they go about their day. (For more information on choosing and working with deities to protect your home, see chapter 3.) When everyone is back in the house, safe and sound for the day, light the candle again and say a word or two of thanks for leading everyone home safely. This daily ritual builds your relationship with deity and keeps a level of protective intent in the room.

You might add a thick binder full of blank pages to your family altar for creating a family book of shadows. Use this to keep track of your sabbat activities, spiritual milestones, and spell work. However, keep in mind that this book can document not only the magical or spiritual practices of the family, but also the activities that bring the family together. Allow each member to add writings, drawings, and photos that they feel are important to remember as well.

Once the family altar is complete, consider this room not only as a place for the family to gather, but also a sacred space that should be treated as such. Keep the clutter down as much as possible, and clean the altar area on a regular basis. Make sure that everyone understands that it is not just a table or a place to leave a soda.

Making the Mundane Magical

Every room in your home is going to have items in it that can be used as magical tools. Some might be obvious, some not so much. Here are a few things you might find in your living room that can enhance your spells and workings.

The Game Closet

Dice: When you need to change your luck, wrap two dice in a scrap of green cloth and carry them in your pocket.

Game pieces: Use game pieces as poppets to represent family members when doing protection magic.

Play money: Hold fake bills in the amount that you need in your hands and say, "Draw to me prosperity, as I will, so mote it be!" Place the fake bills in your wallet until you can replace them with the real thing.

Scrabble tile divination: Lay the tiles facedown on a table while concentrating on your question. Turn over nine tiles and see if they reveal any words, names, or initials that clarify an answer.

Your Desk

The Mail: When you need a quick response to your magical workings, especially if it's something concerning communication, put your magical spell in the mail to help get a swift response from the universe. Address an envelope to yourself and add a stamp. On a piece of paper, write out what you need,

 the mundane steps you've already taken to acquire your goal, and exactly when you need to accomplish it by. Be as detailed as you can. Fold the letter up and place it in the envelope. A pinch of any appropriately corresponding herbs can be added before you seal the envelope up and send it. When the letter comes back to you, don't open it. Instead, place it on your hearthstone and leave it until the magic manifests. When it does, burn the envelope, still unopened, in a heat-safe dish or your cauldron.

Telephone: When you need to get in contact with someone but have been playing phone tag with them or they've been out of touch, write the person's name on a square of paper and place it under your phone.

Shelves

Books: Concentrate on a question you have, and then select a book from your shelves. Set it spine down on a flat surface and allow it to fall open naturally to a random page. With your eyes closed, point to any spot on the page; then read the selection and see how it might apply. This form of divination is called bibliomancy.

Photographs: Use photos for sympathetic magic as you would a poppet for healing, love, or protection magic.

Areas of Magic to Focus On in the Living Room

- Prosperity magic for the good of the household
- Protection magic aimed at the whole home, property, and everyone who lives there
- Ancestral workings
- Healing magic for people or pets

Deities Associated with Living Rooms

Any hearth deities, ancestors, or guardian spirits, including Bes, Brighid, brownies, Hestia, your ancestors by birth or choosing, Saulé, and Zao Jun

THE KITCHEN

Life is a combination of magic and pasta.
—FEDERICO FELLINI

Often considered the heart of the home, the kitchen is perhaps one of the easiest rooms to incorporate into your magical practices. Preparing food is something you probably do every day, whether it's throwing bread in the toaster or spending all day simmering a pot of homemade pasta sauce. No matter your

level of cooking experience or love for food, the time you spend creating a meal can also be spent creating magic.

Each addition to a meal will have its own magical vibrations, so take advantage of them! If you're still learning the correspondences of herbs, think about printing out a few of the ones you use most and hanging them inside the door to your spice cabinet. As you add one to what you are cooking, a simple "I add this (name of herb) for (your intention)" will not only enhance its impact on your desired outcome, but will also keep you more focused on the magical aspect of the cooking process. Once you've learned about the correspondences of foods, herbs, and spices, you can begin to generate entire menus to reinforce whatever enchanted task you are working on. (See chapters 4 and 5 for more information on the magical properties of the items in your kitchen.)

Creating a Kitchen Altar

An altar in your kitchen can be as simple as an image of your chosen deity over your stove, on a shelf, windowsill, or on the inside of a kitchen cabinet. Add a small offering bowl and a candle, and you have all the basics. In my own practice, working with Hestia as my kitchen deity, I have an image of her attached to the inside of a cabinet I can easily leave open when I'm working. This placement protects her from splattering sauces, steam, and the general messiness of a busy kitchen. I keep a candle and a small offering bowl on my cupboard. I light the candle in Hestia's honor whenever I'm working in the kitchen, and the first bit of each meal goes into the offering bowl. If you haven't chosen a particular deity to work with specifically in your kitchen, you can still use a candle as an informal ritual to get you into a more relaxed and focused state of mind before beginning any kitchen work.

Alternatively, you may dedicate your kitchen altar to the spirit of family members passed with whom you might have shared a love of cooking. If your grandmother was the person who first taught you how to make cookies or knead dough, and you can feel her near you when you cook, honor her as an ancestor in your kitchen. A small framed photo, a copy of one of her recipes (laminated to protect it), and a candle in her favorite color or scent make a perfect kitchen altar.

Before you begin creating a meal, take a moment before your altar to center yourself, clear your head, and focus on the meal you are about to prepare. Light the candle, and relax while you cook. Give yourself the time to enjoy what you are doing, appreciate your ingredients, and give thanks that you have the ability to feed your family a great meal. Don't forget to get the whole family involved in the food preparation! This is a great time to talk about your day. When the food is ready to put on the table, snuff out the candle with a few simple words of thanks.

Protecting Sinks and Other Drains

When we think about protecting our homes, we always remember to check our doors and windows. The one thing that's often overlooked is the water drains. These openings lead completely off of our protected property, providing the opportunity for all sorts of energy to wander in. A simple sink cleansing followed by a protection brew can fix this situation right up! Start off by putting a large pot of water on to boil, then turn it down to just a simmer. To the pot add a cup of salt and a handful each of dried sage, rosemary, dill, and thyme. Throw in several pinches of mustard seed and two or three bay leaves. Turn the heat off, and allow the pot to steep for fifteen minutes.

As the herbs steep, pour a cup of baking soda into each of your sinks. Follow this up with a cup of white vinegar, and allow them to foam. When the foaming stops, run hot water down the drain for a few seconds. Not only will this clean your drains and pipes, but it will also help clear away any small clogs!

Now that the drains are cleansed, strain your pot of herbs into a clean pot. Discard the spent herbs; then add the juice of two lemons to the herbal infusion and mix. Pour a cup of this brew down each of your drains. Don't forget to flush a bit down each toilet and pour some into the bottom of your dishwasher.

Ritual Hand Washing

Many Pagans use ritual bathing as a preparation for solitary or group activities. In your everyday practice, I doubt you'll find time to do this before every bit of magic you partake in! A simple alternative is to keep a spray bottle in your kitchen full of your favorite herbal infusion, flower water, or Florida water (see chapter 4 for how to make your own). Taking a moment to ritually cleanse your hands and draw a few deep breaths can help not only center you throughout the day, but also remind you that even the most unglamorous tasks honor deity and your family. If you are feeling stressed out or put upon, add a small prayer to your hand cleansing, such as, "Lord and Lady, help me remember that it is an honor to be a parent. My actions honor you as well as my family." One of my favorites—that I use more often than I'd like to admit—is "Lord and Lady, please help me keep my temper and remind me why I love this houseful of crazies."

You can use this ritual wash to spray the air as a quick fix to get rid of negative energies after an argument or when you've had someone unpleasant in your home for a visit. Experiment with different scents and combinations until you've created a signature blend that's just right for you and your household.

Kitchen Book of Shadows

In starting a book of shadows for your kitchen, you will not only have a record of the magical works done in that space, but you can also create a treasured record of memories spent with friends and family over meals shared in good times. To this book add culinary herb correspondences, information about your kitchen deities, family secret recipes, recipe clippings from magazines, and notes about social gatherings held in your home. The first page of the book might be filled in with a blessing, borrowed or created, such as "In this book, my recipes reside, traditions and memories locked inside. I ask that this book be blessed from above, and all created with it be filled with love."

Kitchen Tool Cleansing

When purchasing new pots, pans, or utensils to add to a kitchen, we normally give the item a good wash and a rinse and set to using it. If we stop and think, however, about all the places that tool has traveled, all the hands it has passed through, and all the energy it has potentially picked up, we realize it might need a little more than just a soap and water scrub. Considering that we might be using these tools every single day to create the food our family eats, a bit more of a magical cleansing might be beneficial!

It's simple enough to give them a more substantial wash. While filling the sink with very warm water, add your regular dish detergent, a handful of salt, the juice of half a lemon, and a sprig of rosemary. Allow your new kitchen tools to soak for 15 minutes, give them a good scrubbing and a rinse in hot water. For new appliances, wipe them down inside and out with a vinegar- or lemon-based cleaning spray made for kitchen appliances.

Making a Kitchen Cabinet Abundance Jar

It is said that maintaining a supply of both salt and alfalfa in your kitchen will keep your cupboards from ever being bare. Follow these steps to create an abundance jar with these two key ingredients.

Items Needed:

- A small jar
- Kosher salt
- A few coins
- Alfalfa

1. Take a small jar and fill half full with kosher salt.

2. Add a few coins (pennies are fine) to the jar, then fill the remainder of the jar with alfalfa. (You can usually find alfalfa in grocery stores or pet stores near the small creature sections.)

3. Screw the lid on tightly. Holding the jar in your hands, visualize your cupboards, pantry, and refrigerator full of healthy foods and say,

Bless this home with abundance. May it always be filled with enough to share. So mote it be!

4. Place the jar to the back of a shelf and let it be. Once a year, refill the jar and restate the prayer.

5. To strengthen the blessing on your home, make sure to take an item or two from your own shelves each month to donate to a local food pantry or soup kitchen.

◆ ◆ ◆

Making the Mundane Magical

The kitchen holds a treasure trove of items just waiting to be used as magical tools. With such a wide variety of objects, from cleaning supplies to cooking utensils, almost everything you need for your magical practice is right at your fingertips!

Kitchen Supplies and Tools

Broom: Brooms are used in various magical practices around the world. The easiest way to incorporate a cleaning broom into your daily measures is to purchase one with a handle made of wood and carve a spell right into it. If you can't find a wood-handled broom, it's easy enough to write on another type with a permanent marker. My own broom contains the carved words "I sweep in love, luck, and prosperity. I sweep out all negativity." Whenever I grab my broom, I say the words aloud before I start sweeping.

French press: If tea is not your thing, brew up a batch of coffee in a French press and practice casseomancy, or coffee ground reading. A French press is also perfect for easy brewing and straining of herbs to add to washes.

Kitchen shears: Keep a pair of kitchen shears separate from your other cooking shears to use as you would a boline (a magical knife), for cutting herbs, strings, or other materials that you'll be using specifically for magic.

Kitchen twine: Kitchen twine is handy for more than just trussing up a chicken. Cut a length to tie off mojo bags or to do a quick bit of knot magic.

Plastic sandwich bags: Need a break from someone who's become an energy leech? Place their image or a piece of paper with their name written on it into a baggies and seal. Put it in the freezer and leave undisturbed until you're ready to deal with them again.

Pots and pans: A small cast-iron pot from the cooking section of your local department store is often much less expensive than a cauldron and, for those without a metaphysical shop nearby, much easier to find.

Sponge: Sponges are fairly inexpensive and make a great tool for so many things. Use your imagination to find ways to make good use of them. Finances drying up? Cut a circle out of a sponge and draw a dollar sign on it with a permanent marker. Keep this "coin" in the kitchen, near your sink, and make sure to keep it wet until the money starts flowing in again. Know someone you need to cut out of your life? Write their name on one side of a sponge, yours on the other. Cut the sponge in half between the two names. Toss their side out in the garbage. If you aren't comfortable throwing it out, drop it off on the edge of their property instead.

Teapot and teacups: Brew up a big pot of loose tea leaves and practice the art of tea leaf reading (tasseomancy).

Tinfoil: Wrap herbs in tinfoil and then mold it into an appropriate shape. This is perfect for a quick protection spell: Add garlic, basil, and salt to a square of foil and fold into a small envelope. Use a pencil to write the name of the person you're protecting onto the packet. To speed the spell along, place it in a heated oven until the herbs become fragrant. Remove carefully and set aside in a safe place.

Wooden spoons: Use them as you would a wand or athame to focus energy.

Junk Drawer Divination

Everyone has that one drawer for everything in the world that has no other place to be. Go through it to find odds and ends to create your own personal divination set. In a small bag or box, collect items that represent different concepts for you. As you add each to the box, tell it what it represents. For example, if you're adding a cork to represent celebrations, say something like, "I name you celebration. You represent a future party or get-together with family and friends." Write each meaning down in a notebook. When you start practicing reading with your set, write down the results in the same notebook to refer back to later. To do a reading, add something to the bag to represent yourself or the person you are reading for, such as a button or a small character figure from an old game. Ask a question, then tilt the bag over and spill the contents out onto a flat surface. The closer an item falls to the item signifying the person, the more important that item is. Alternately, just draw one item from the bag to answer the question. Here are a few things found in my divination bag and what they represent to me.

- **Cork:** Cheerfulness or a festive get-together.

- **Ring:** Represents a commitment to something or someone.

- **Coin:** Coming prosperity or good luck when heads up, a loss when heads down.

- **Matchstick:** A good omen. If any unlucky objects are near it, it voids them.

- **Key:** A new beginning or the opening or unlocking of something.

- **Toy car (or small toy train):** When close to the item that represents the person you are reading for, it represents an accident. When farther away, it represents travel or a long journey.

Objects can represent whatever you want them to; just assign each one a meaning and be consistent in using that meaning for it.

Areas of Magic to Focus On in the Kitchen

- Love
- Prosperity
- Harmony
- Any cooking, food or herb magic

Deities Associated with the Kitchen

Deities of cooking, fire, hearths, food, or herbs such as Agni, Airmid, Brighid, Hestia, Kaya nu Hima, or Zao Jun

THE LAUNDRY ROOM

I wish we could wash from our hearts and our souls
The strains of the week away,
And let water and air by their magic make
Ourselves as pure as they.
Then on the earth there would be indeed,
A glorious washing day!

—LOUISA MAY ALCOTT

Laundry has always been one of my most dreaded chores. It's a never-ending battle, load after load. It isn't even the actual washing that will get you, it's all that folding and putting away. This is where the clever domestic witch gets her family involved very early on; even the youngest of kids can fold washcloths and pull out socks to be paired. Invest in plenty of baskets and hampers, and get everyone used to putting their dirty clothes in and putting them away immediately after they've been washed.

Whether you are lucky enough to have a designated room to sort and wash in, whether your washer and dryer are tucked into a corner of another room, or even if you have to haul your clothes to a communal laundry, there are plenty of things you can do to take this chore from mundane to magical. The laundry area is actually a pretty balanced area to do magical works, as it encompasses all of the elements: the washer is a tool of Water, the dryer contains both Fire and Air, and that basket of dirty clothes? Definitely some Earth in that.

Start your laundry room magic with the basic tools: the washer and dryer. Treat these as you would any of your other magical tools by keeping them and the area around them clean and in good repair. If you have a specific room or area for laundry, give it a good cleansing with soap and water or a cleansing wash from chapter 4. If the room has a window, open it up and give the room a good airing while you clean. Rid the area of any garbage sitting around and get organized. Gather your laundry baskets and give them a good wipe down as well.

While you tidy and straighten, give a bit of thought to how important clothing and laundry are in our lives. Doesn't it feel great to slip into clean pajamas after a bath, a comfy blanket when we are ill, or a warm sweater when the weather turns chilly? We don't give much thought or thanks day to day for something as simple as having clean clothes, but today, consider how blessed you are to have them and to have the ability to easily maintain them.

Once you've gathered all of these tools into your work space, perform a consecration to dedicate your laundry space. What follows is a simple ritual that can be performed in a short amount of time and with very simple tools.

Laundry Room Consecration

Change your ideas about the dreaded laundry room! Consecrate it as a sacred place and dedicate it to your favorite deity. From here on out, work on seeing the room as a place where you honor your patron—not only by participating in your family's chores, but also as a place to teach your children to be independent and self-sufficient!

Items Needed:

- A white candle in a holder and something to light it with
- A small dish of salt
- A small dish of water
- A bit of incense (optional)

1. When you have a few moments to yourself, sit quietly in your laundry room space. Take a few cleansing breaths while thinking about how you are creating a sacred space in which you and your family can clean your clothing. When you feel centered, calm, and ready, begin.

2. Light the candle and say,

   On this day and by Fire, I consecrate this room as a sacred space.

3. Hold the dish of salt and either sprinkle a bit of it in the corners of the room or sprinkle a bit at each corner of your washer and dryer. While you do this, say,

   On this day and by Earth, I consecrate this room as a sacred space.

4. Take the dish of water, dip your fingers into it and either sprinkle a few drops around the room traveling clockwise, or use your wetted fingers

to trace your favorite runes or symbols around the room. While you're working, repeat,

On this day and by Water, I consecrate this room as a sacred space.

5. For the element of Air, the only tool you need is your body and its ability to blow air into each corner of the room. If you prefer, light up a bit of incense and blow or wave the smoke around your space while you say,

On this day and by Air, I consecrate this room as a sacred space.

6. Finish your ritual by standing in the center of the room and saying aloud,

This room is now consecrated. I ask for it to be blessed by the Lord and Lady (or your chosen deity) as a sacred space where I will work for the good of myself, my family, and deity.

7. A god or goddess can be chosen to look over the room if one appeals to you, or you feel so called. Deities or guardian spirits that are associated with the elements of Fire or Air are appropriate in this space, as could any deity associated with the home or domestic arts.

8. Consider Saulé (Sow-Lay), a Baltic hearth goddess connected to both sun and sky who watches over domestic work. The goddess Mokosz (Moh-Kosh) from Poland has been known to help out with laundry chores when pleased with offerings left by her followers.

◆ ◆ ◆

Creating an Altar

Depending on the size of your space, you could create a simple altar on a shelf or you could hang a photo of a chosen deity over your work space.

Constructing an altar collage is also an option; gather photos or drawings of a chosen deity, small representations of their symbols, and anything you feel is appropriate. Paste them on card stock or in a shadow box and hang on the wall. Add a small offering bowl and offer a few small fruits (grapes are great for this) or veggies. When they start to look past their prime, toss them outside for the neighborhood critters. Let the shrine be a reminder that laundry doesn't have to be drudgery, but it can be a sacred or magical experience.

Magic in the Laundry Room

When you've gotten your new sacred space all set up, it's time for a bit of magic! When you're looking to change the energy in your home or around those in it, the laundry is a great place to start.

Incorporating essential oils into your laundry magic is an easy way to do this. Find an essential oil that fits your intentions and simply dab a few drops onto an old washcloth or sock before adding it to the wash. The oil will disperse through the load, sharing its vibrations with everything it touches. Unfortunately, essential oils can be a bit expensive. If you don't have the right one in stock, it's time to hit the spice rack.

Adding a bundle of herbs to the wash can provide just the vibrations you need. Place the herbs in the toe of an old, clean sock and tie it shut, put the herbs in an organza bag and tie it closed, or sew herbs into a square of material recycled from an old cotton shirt. Throw the bundle in with your wash and transfer it to the dryer with the clothes. With a few words to enforce your intention, you can create a great batch of magical laundry.

Peaceful sleep load: Want to bring calm and a better night's sleep to the family? Tie a couple of chamomile tea bags into an old sock and throw it in with the sheets. As the water starts to fill the washer, repeat the following:

> *Chamomile work as a balm; bring to my family peace and calm!*

Prosperity load: Sew a bit of basil into a square of green cloth and add it to a load of your work clothes. While the washer fills with water, say:

> *Basil, basil, draw to me business success and prosperity!*

Say this again as you transfer the clothes to the dryer.

Here are a few more chants to get you started. You can either say them alone, or add an herb bundle to go with them for a little extra oomph.

> *As I wash this load of clothes*
> *I wash away our troubles and woes.*

◆ ◆ ◆

> *Goddess, these troubles*
> *To you I have told;*
> *Wash them away*
> *With this water so cold.*

◆ ◆ ◆

Goddess this bad luck
I scrub with these jeans,
Away dirt and troubles
As this water it cleans!

Don't forget to offer a few simple words of thanks to deity or the universe when you remove the clothes from the dryer for folding. If you are using an herb bundle, it will last for one more load before you untie and empty it. If you're using a recycled scrap of cloth for your bundle, after that it can just be thrown away.

Another way to honor deity is to make your laundry more energy efficient to minimize your impact on the earth. Simple ways to do this include:

- Running your washer and dryer only when you have a full load

- Running several loads in a row to take advantage of the fact that your dryer is already warmed up

- Hanging your clothes outside on a clothesline when the weather permits

- Cleaning out your lint trap after every dryer load

- Turning down your water heater to 120°F. This will save energy (and money) on every load and keep your family safe from accidental scalding.

Making the Mundane Magical

We may spend more time in the laundry room than we'd like, but opening your eyes to the magical uses of what the room holds could make your time there a bit more magical.

Fabric sheets: When you have the need to keep someone or something from latching on to you, or want some help shedding a bad habit, write down exactly what you want to release and wrap it up in a fabric sheet. Hold it closed with a clothespin or a piece of string, and say, "Don't cling to me, let me be. Release, release this negativity."

Stain stick: If you are looking to make something disappear from your life, write it out with a stain removing stick or pen on a scrap piece of cloth and throw it in with a load of wash using hot water.

Areas of Magic to Focus On in the Laundry Room

- Cleansings or banishment
- Adding intent to clothes or linens

Deities Associated with the Laundry Room

Deities of water, of washing or cleansing, or of the domestic arts, such as Asherah, Mokosz, or Saulé

BATHROOM

There must be quite a few things that a hot bath won't cure,
but I don't know many of them.
—SYLVIA PLATH

The bathroom is the ideal spot for all sorts of cleansing and purification baths. The simplest option of all is just taking a quick shower while visualizing the water

washing away all negativity from your body. Almost any culinary herb can safely be made into a tea, strained and added to your bath to infuse the water with whatever intent you're looking for. There are also plenty of other items in the bathroom besides the tub and shower that can be applied in a variety of ways.

Making the Mundane Magical

Besides cleansing baths and showers, there are some great finds for your magical practice in the bathroom. Here are a few ideas to get you started.

Bandages: Plain bandages can always be used in a simple healing ritual. Just write the person's name on the bandage and place it under a blue candle. Light the candle and allow it to burn as long as you can. There are a wide variety of character bandages on the market these days, so look for any that you might be able to use in a more creative way. Superhero bandages are great for a little protection magic; faeries can be used in wish magic; and bandages with hearts on them are great for a little heartbreak management.

Brushes or combs: These can "detangle" you from a situation or person.

Cotton balls: Cotton is said to bring good luck. If you are feeling in need of a change in your luck, carry a cotton ball in your pocket. Keep one in your wallet to change your luck with money. Burning cotton is said to bring rain.

Cotton swabs: Cotton swabs are good for more than cleaning out ears physically. You can also use them in a simple communication spell to help clean out someone's ears so that they will be more willing to hear what you need to say to them. Take a fine-pointed pen and write the name of the person you need to listen to you on the swab. Hold it in your hands and say, "Hear me speak, mind my word. Clean your ears so I'll be heard!" Place the swab somewhere it won't be disturbed until after you have your talk.

Soap: Need to wash a bad habit out of your life? Carve its name deeply into a bar of soap. Use the soap every day when you shower until the word is unrecognizable, and then throw it away.

Toilet paper: Nothing is better for a quick banishment spell than a roll of toilet paper and your toilet. Write down anything you would like to banish from your life—such as negativity, a bad habit, debt, or illness—onto the paper, wad it up, and flush it away.

Areas of Magic to Focus On in the Bathroom

- Banishing
- Cleansing

Deities Associated with Bathrooms

Deities of water, cleansing, or beauty such as Aglaia, Aphrodite, Sulis, Temazcalteci, Venus

CHILDREN'S BEDROOMS

While we try to teach our children about life, our children teach us what life is all about.
—ANGELA SCHWINDT

A child's room should be a haven for them. It should be a private place where they can relax, store their most treasured items, and get away from it all. Help

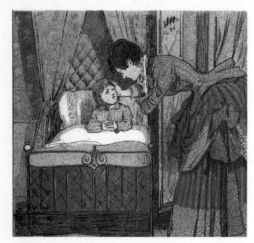

your children understand from a young age that keeping their own room clean is not only their responsibility, but it also ensures their privacy, since mom or dad won't have to come in hunting for dishes or dirty clothes.

When your children are small, you can set up an altar in their rooms on an out of reach shelf. It might contain representations of a deity that watches over children, protective talismans, or items to help ensure good health. As each child grows old enough to take a real interest in such things, work with them to create a sacred space at their own

level. There are shops easily found online that produce child-safe representations of various gods and goddesses, or you can make your own versions with scraps of cloth or felt.

The older a child gets, the more likely he or she will want to take over the practices at this altar. Help them by providing age-appropriate tools and books and setting a good example with how you care for your own spiritual and magical items.

A Children's Book of Shadows

You can start a child's book of shadows for them as soon as you know a baby is on the way. Include any rituals or spells conducted for the child during pregnancy, information on their birth, and good wishes or blessings from family members and friends. Until the child is old enough to care for the book properly, keep it put up and add to it yourself as spiritual or magical events happen through their younger years. When they reach an age at which they can take over the book for themselves, encourage them to write down their dreams, experiences with nature, and goals as well as journaling their troubles and what steps (magical and mundane) that they have taken to fix them.

Quick Magical Protection of Children

Keeping our children safe has to be one of the top worries of any family. While we teach them all the mundane ways to watch out for danger, there are many magical ways to help ensure their safety as well.

- Hang or draw symbols of protection over the doorway and around the windows of the child's room. A simple and subtle way to do this is with a white crayon.

- Purchase a set of glow in the dark stick-on stars for the ceiling. Before hanging them up, use a permanent marker to draw runes or protective sigils on them.

- Create a protection poppet. Trace the shape of a gingerbread man cookie cutter onto a folded scrap of cloth. Turn the "good" sides toward each other, and sew them up along the edges, leaving a small opening. Turn the figure right side out, then stuff it with a combination of protective herbs and pillow stuffing, before sewing it shut. The poppet can sit in the child's own room or on the family altar.

- Use a marker to draw runes or other protective symbols onto the tags of their clothing or on the bottom of their shoes.

Nightmare Prevention

I'm asked how to help a child who's going through a period of nightmares at least once a month. Many children and even adults have nightmares for a variety of reasons, such as changes in home life, a traumatic event, illness, and sometimes for no obvious reason at all. Whatever the cause, there are few things that can disrupt a household more than scary, sleepless nights and watching your child suffer.

So what do you do about them? Assuming you've taken all the mundane steps to make sure there are no physical or emotional reasons for the nightmares, there are several folk magic remedies to try. Sew up a small sleep pillow from scraps of cloth and include inside a handful of herbs for protection and restful sleep. Before retiring for the night, smudge your child and his or her room with a dried thyme bundle. Native American tradition holds that a dream catcher hung over or near the bed will help stop bad dreams, while Islamic folklore puts its money on eating seven dates every morning to keep nightmares at bay. A bundle of fresh rosemary sprigs in a glass of water adds protection to a room at the same time that it wards off bad dreams.

If you want to put more of the power to stop nightmares in your child's hands, teach them about the Asian guardian Baku. Though more modern depictions of Baku look like a tapir, older versions show him as a hybrid animal—mixing dog, bear, horse, lion, ox, and elephant. This strange looking guardian creature literally lives off of bad dreams. He is invoked upon waking up by calling out to him to eat the bad dreams. Shouting out "Devour my dream, Baku!" is said to bring Baku to a child's side to take away his or her bad dreams. Not only does Baku take the dreams away, but he also leaves good fortune in their place.

Encourage your child to seek out Baku by adding a stuffed Baku to their room or putting up an image of him somewhere in the room. You can also embroider his name onto pillowcases.

Making the Mundane Magical

A child's room is usually already filled with magic and imagination. It doesn't require much to find an item or two that can be taken to the next level and used as a magical tool.

Doctor kits: Use in health and healing spells.

Fashion dolls or action figures: Use as poppets for doing healing or protection magic for people.

Favorite blanket or piece of clothing: Use to create a selection of drawstring bags that your child can use when doing work for him- or herself through the years. The fact that it was worn or well loved will help create a strong connection for the magic to work with.

- Lost teeth or hair clippings: Save hair from a first haircut and lost baby teeth. These can be used in all manner of protection and healing charms as the child grows.

- Old baby clothes: Save a baby sock or two for future fertility spells.

- Stuffed animals: Use as poppets when doing healing or protection magic for pets.

Areas of Magic to Focus On in Children's Bedrooms

- Protection

- Healing

Deities Associated with Children's Bedrooms

Deities associated with the protection of children or families, such as Berchta, Bes, Kishimo-Jin, or Mama Quilla.

ADULT BEDROOMS

There is no remedy for love but to love more.
—HENRY DAVID THOREAU

Whether a family is led by a couple in a committed relationship or a single parent, an adult bedroom should be a place of privacy. Teach kids early on to knock on the door before entering—and show them the same respect when visiting them in their rooms. A bedroom should be a place to relax, be comfortable, and hopefully a spot for a little romance. Keep the space clear of clutter, keep laundry in the hamper and off the floor, and add little touches to make it an inviting place to spend a bit of time. We never seem to have enough time in our bedrooms alone or with our partner, so make sure the time you do spend there is comfy.

A Couple's Book of Shadows

A couple's book of shadows should be a private book, kept away from curious eyes. Start it off by adding all those little important dates such as first dates, the day of a proposal, and the anniversary of your wedding or handfasting. Add any rituals or spells you've worked as a couple to move forward as a more committed partnership or a family. Most important, let the book be a place to leave each other small messages of love, encouragement, and support on a regular basis. The book should be a record of your love, passion, and friendship.

Keeping Things Sexy Spell

As the years go by, as children join the family, and as schedules get more and more complicated, passion can sometimes start to take a backseat to all the other things going on in your life. If you find that you want to try to heat things up a bit, use this simple spell.

1. Grab a pair of your sexiest underwear and a pair of your partner's.

2. Lay out one pair and sprinkle them with dried red rose petals.

3. Lay the next pair on top, then fold them into a small bundle. Wrap them tight with a red ribbon or cord, tying three knots while saying,

   Knot of one, bring on the fun. Second knot to get things hot. Knot of three, passionate sex for me and thee.

4. Place the bundle under the bed. Then make the effort to hit the hay before you're too exhausted to do anything about it!

◆ ◆ ◆

Attracting a New Partner

For those single heads of the household who find themselves ready to settle down with a partner but not spotting any prospects yet, try this simple candle spell — then keep your eyes open!

Items Needed:

- A pen or pencil
- A piece of paper
- A red taper or pillar candle in a safe holder

- Grapeseed oil
- Equal parts dried red, pink, and yellow rose petals, ground fine (for passion, romantic love, and friendship)
- A sheet of tinfoil or waxed foil to spread the ground flowers on
- A lighter or matches

1. Sit in a quiet spot and think about all the qualities you'd like to find in a partner. Concentrate on personality traits, mutual interests that you consider a necessity, and things that really matter in a long-term relationship. Write all of these things down in as much detail as you can. Add a list of places where you think you might meet someone with those traits. Fold the paper in half and set it aside.

2. Take the candle in hand and hold it for a few minutes, concentrating on the traits that you wrote on your paper. Then think about traits of your own that will make you a good partner and what you might need to work on a bit (be honest!).

3. Wet your fingers with a bit of the grapeseed oil, and dress the candle, rubbing the oil on from the bottom up, all around the candle. Be careful to avoid getting oil on the wick. When the candle has been dressed all the way around, roll it in the ground flower petals to cover. Set the candle in the holder and place your folded list underneath. Light the candle while saying,

   Candle of love, candle of fire, help to bring my heart's desire.

4. Light the candle for a few minutes each day, watching carefully, as dressed candles can sometimes flare.

5. Get yourself out and about so that you have more opportunities to meet that special someone!

◆ ◆ ◆

Areas of Magic to Focus On in Adult Bedrooms

- Love
- Lust

- Commitment

- Fidelity

Deities Associated with Adult Bedrooms

Deities of love, lust, beauty, or marriage. The Chinese spirits (Lord) Ch'uang-Kung and (Lady) Ch'uang-Mu are said to decide what goes on in bed.

Creating magical space in each room of your home can take some time and effort, but it's well worth it. Home is where we spend much of the quality time of our lives away from work and school, nestled away from the rest of the world. It's our sanctuary and should be a joy for us to walk into. Creating sacred space in each room and tending to it on a daily basis open up the channels in our home, giving positive energy a path to flow freely. I've found that since I've created these spaces throughout my house, it has produced a more calming atmosphere that allows me to breathe more deeply. It's definitely allowed me to enjoy my home and the things associated with it so much more!

two

Air, Earth, Water, and Fire: Elements for the Domestic Witch

We all know the four elements: Air, Earth, Water, Fire. Some of us call them to our magical rituals. We seek places where we can find them in perfect balance. How many of us take advantage of them in our everyday lives, though?

Just as it is important to have balance in your magical workings, it's also important to have balance in your home. Simply adding a representation of each element to each room can help, but it might not be enough. In trying to bring an emotional, calming equilibrium to your household, you must consider each room individually. What type of energy does the room have already? What type of energy would you like to promote in that area? What can you move into or out of the room to help create a space that is comfortable for all who enter it?

The elements aren't just powers to be called or something to be found in perfect combination at your local beach. They are all around us, both in their simplest form and in forms we might not recognize at first. Below is a roundup of each element and information on how you can use them around your home. Remember that just having them in the room will not make as big an impact as recognizing their actual use in the room on a daily basis. Acknowledge the elements silently to yourself when you walk into a room; this will help strengthen their magical effects.

AIR

Air is all around us of course. We need it to breathe; we enjoy its coolness when it blows gently in the summer; we see its power in storms. This element rules over communication of all sorts, creativity, studying, writing, and some forms of divination. A tool of Air is a good addition to any room regularly used for studying and homework. Place a tool of Air on the dinner table to promote family conversations. If you have a room in your home that makes you feel sluggish or apathetic, an influx of air can encourage more mental acuity and energy.

Household Representations of Air

- air conditioners and vents
- air popper for popcorn
- blenders
- ceiling fans
- clotheslines or racks
- dish drainers
- dust mops
- exhaust fans on stoves
- feather dusters
- hair dryers
- handheld fans

- kites, statues of windmills

- mail

- pinwheels

- vacuums

- whisks

- whistles

- wind chimes

- wind instruments

- wooden spoons when used as wands

As you get more comfortable recognizing everyday household objects as tools of magic, start to build upon what you know about the element each represents to create your own magical spells or rituals for using them; the simpler the better, in my opinion. Create a fun chant or song to sing as you run the vacuum through the house, or you could try:

> *Tool of Air, I dance with you*
> *In my home, 'neath the Goddesses' view!*
> *I tidy and clean, the whole house through*
> *Spic-and-span 'til it's like brand-new!*

Don't just push the vacuum around begrudgingly, really do dance it around your house! Let loose and have fun!

Areas of the Home That Represent Air

Laundry room, porch, deck, balconies, any upper level floors, attics, any east-facing doors or windows

Simple Ways to Add Air Around Your Home

- Create an Air altar on an eastern-facing wall.

- Build your clothesline on the east side of your home.

- Hang wind chimes or a witch's ladder containing feathers off your porch or near your front door.

- Pick up a few tiny painted wooden ladybugs from the craft store and hide them around the house.

- Create a charm bag with three or nine herbs associated with Air. Hang it in the corner of your house closest to true north to invite this element into your home.

- Open east-facing windows and let in the breeze, especially at dawn.

- Hang yellow, white, or pastel colors in the dining room to encourage conversation over dinner, or in the study to help with memory retention.

- Create an altar to a deity whose element is Air.

Deities Related to Air

Goddesses of Air: Aura, Hepit, Hera, Marici, Nut

Gods of Air: Aether, Amun-Ra, Caelus, Horus, Lelantos, Shango, Shu, Ukko

Spirits and Mythical Creatures of Air: Archangel Raphael, gryphons, Pegasus, sylphs

For the Kids

Air is one of the easiest and most fun tools to teach children about. Lie down out in the yard and have them close their eyes and feel the breeze on their faces; look up and find shapes in the clouds. Grab a kite and take it for a spin! Consider creating an "element box" for them, and add a feather, a pennywhistle, or a pinwheel to represent Air. Let them help you create a meal or snack using just foods associated with air.

Foods Associated with Air

Cake, green grapes, jelly, maple syrup, meringue, pie crusts, popcorn, puff pastries, scrambled eggs, soufflé, steamed vegetables, whipped cream, yeast breads, yellow foods

Culinary Herbs and Plants Associated with Air

Allspice, anise seeds, bergamot, caraway, cardamom, chicory, dandelion, dill, hops, lavender, lemongrass, maple, marjoram, mint, oregano, parsley, pine, rosemary, sage, spearmint, star anise

Drinks Associated with Air

Herbal teas, juice, wine

On a day when you especially need to communicate well with others, start off with a breakfast of scrambled eggs topped with parsley, toast with natural grape jelly, juice, and coffee with a dollop of whipped cream on top. Go through what you need to say while slowly eating and concentrating on each bite of food.

EARTH

The element of Earth rules over growth, business, money, fertility, grounding and centering, and all things to do with planting and gardening. Add tools or representations of earth to any room in which you do business or create things for sale, to the bedroom if you are trying to conceive, or to any room where arguments tend to pop up on a regular basis.

Household Representations of Earth

- bamboo screens or blinds
- brooms with wooden handles
- gardening tools
- hardwood floors
- houseplants
- modeling clay
- natural fabrics
- paper

- soil

- spice racks

- stone tiles

- terra-cotta dishes or pots

- toilet paper

- wooden blocks

- wooden furniture

- wood for fireplaces

Most homes have an abundance of representations of Earth. Pick one that you use or handle on a regular basis to help promote the energy of Earth within your home. You could change the vacuum chant in the previous section to "Tool of Earth" to use while you wield your broom through the house, or if you have wooden floors in your home, chant as you clean them:

> I cleanse and bless this wooden floor,
> From the front of the house 'round to the back door.
> Help us ground, keep us stable,
> Focused, centered, strong and able!

Areas of the Home That Represent Earth

North-facing doors or windows, mudrooms, the garage, sandboxes, greenhouses, window boxes

Simple Ways to Add Earth Around Your Home

- Add a jar of earth from your yard or garden to any room that needs a bit of grounding.

- Throw a pinch of soil from your yard into prosperity charms.

- If you've been having trouble focusing, carry a stone from your garden in your pocket.

- Place plants in terra-cotta pots throughout the house.

- Fill a small basket with natural objects from your yard, such as pine-cones, stones, and dried herbs.

Deities Related to Earth

Goddesses of Earth: Anu, Auxo, Blodeuwudd, Ceres, Demeter, Gaia, Karpo, Pachamama, Persephone

Gods of Earth: Geb, The Green Man, The Horned God, Hou Tu, Ten-Ten-Vilu

Spirits and Mythical Creatures of Earth: Archangel Uriel, gnomes

For the Kids

Take the kids outside to dig in the dirt or the garden. While you're out there, make mud pies, or do crafts with clay. Start a rock collection. Teach the kids how to bake bread or make peanut butter.

Foods Associated with Earth

Bread, peanut butter, salt

Culinary Herbs and Plants Associated with Earth

Alfalfa, barley, beets, buckwheat, corn, marjoram, oats, peanuts, potato, rye, tarragon, wheat, yeast

Drinks Associated with Earth

Beer

WATER

Water rules over dreams, emotions, healing, the ability to adapt, and cleansings. It can be a tricky element to incorporate around the house: too much of it, and a room can become a hotbed of emotions; too little, and an atmosphere can be created lacking in compassion and empathy.

Household Representations of Water

- bathtubs
- beach balls
- clothes washer
- coffeepots and teakettles
- cups
- dishwasher
- empty bottles
- fishing poles
- fish tanks
- garden hoses
- glasses
- gravy boats
- lighthouse figures
- nets
- oars
- pet bowls
- pitchers
- pools
- rain barrels
- rain boots or raincoats
- rubber ducks
- sauce pans
- scrub brushes and sponges
- seashells

- showers

- sinks

- umbrellas

- watering cans

If you find your family arguing repeatedly in the same room, look around and see if there are any water-based items you can remove. Leave them in another room for a week, and see if there is any change in the atmosphere.

Areas of the Home That Represent Water

West-facing doors or windows, bathrooms, kitchen, laundry room

Simple Ways to Add Water Around Your Home

- Add seashells or sea glass to your altar or pile them in a vase.

- Add a fishing net to the corner of a room near the ceiling to hold stuffed animals or extra throw pillows.

- Use an old, colorful rain boot to hold umbrellas near the front door.

- Place a collection of blue-tinted bottles on the windowsill of a west-facing window.

Deities Related to Water

Goddesses of Water: Aphrodite, Doris, Eurynome, Mazu, Ochun, Saulé, Vedenomo, Venus, Yemaya

Gods of Water: Agwé, Lir, Neptune, Oceanus, Olocun, Poseidon, Tlaloc

Spirits and Mythical Creatures of Water: Archangel Gabriel, Crinaeae, hippocampi, kelpie, mermaids, naiads, Nix, Pegaeae, undine

For the Kids

Nothing is better on a hot summer day than a lesson on the element of Water! Take a trip to the beach or the community pool or break out the water guns.

Have a water balloon fight. In cooler weather, fill up the tub and race boats or rubber ducks.

Foods Associated with Water

Anchovies, butter, cheese, chocolate, eggs, fish, honey, milk, sea salt, sushi

Culinary Herbs and Plants Associated with Water

Aloe vera, apple, apricot, artichokes, avocado, banana, blackberry, blueberry, broccoli, brussels sprouts, cabbage, chamomile, lemon, lemongrass, melons, nori, poppy seeds, soy, sugar, tamarind, thyme

Drinks Associated with Water

Ale, fruit juice, mead, tea, wine

FIRE

Fire rules all the passionate things in life, such as love, sex, romance, and change. It also influences courage, enthusiasm, purification, new beginnings, and banishings. Be sure to have at least one Fire-related item in your bedroom to keep things spicy!

Household Representations of Fire

- candles
- clothes dryer
- electric outlets
- fireplaces
- grills
- hair dryers
- heaters
- heating vents

- hot plates

- iron and ironing board

- lamps

- lava lamps

- lighters

- matches

- microwaves

- ovens

- overhead lighting

- pilot light

- stoves

In colder months, honoring the element of Fire is as easy as consciously turning on your home's heater or lighting a fire in the fireplace. In warmer months, don't give up on working with this element daily. When turning on a burner or plugging something into an outlet, you can acknowledge Fire with a heartfelt, "Hail, Fire!"

Areas of the Home That Represent Fire

Rooms containing fireplaces, the kitchen, south-facing windows

Simple Ways to Add Fire Around Your Home

- Hang strings of lights around a room.

- Place candles around the house.

- Hang up a string of dried hot chili peppers.

Deities Related to Fire

Goddesses of Fire: Brighid, Chantico, Gabija, Hestia, Oya, Pele, Vesta

Gods of Fire: Agni, Belenus, Hephaestus, Prometheus, Sutr, Vulcan

Spirits and Mythical Creatures of Fire: Archangel Michael, dragons, phoenix, salamanders

For the Kids

Fire can be a bit trickier to explore with children. Most activities will require close parental supervision. Create a volcano together. Practice cooking or making candles. Roast marshmallows or turkey dogs over a fire pit or grill.

Foods Associated with Fire

Artichoke, arugula, asparagus, olives, olive oil, onion, orange

Culinary Herbs and Plants Associated with Fire

Basil, bay leaf, black pepper, cayenne, chili peppers, chives, cilantro, cinnamon, clove, coriander, cumin, dill, fennel seed, flax, garlic, ginger, mustard seed, nutmeg, peppermint, sesame

Drinks Associated with Fire

Coffee

three

Domestic Deities and Household Guardian Spirits

Every domestic witch will eventually look into the subject of finding a household deity. Traditionally, there are two types of domestic deities: a major god or goddess or the minor or local entities called animistic deities. You've probably heard of at least a few of the goddesses associated with the household: Hestia, Frigg, or Brighid are some of the most popular today. But have you heard of the tomte, domovoi, or cofgodas? These are but a few of the animistic deities that have been worshipped in the past.

Domestic deities look out for the members of the household, the home itself, and/or the land around the home as well as any animals or livestock that live on it. In ancient days, a household would represent its deity with a small idol: a statue, a painting, or even an amulet. Wealthy households dedicated shrines to their deity. The deity was held in the highest esteem and treated as part of the family. Often they were invited to eat with the family, with plates of food left out for them in offering, sometimes at the family's table, sometimes tucked away in a spot where the deity was thought to frequent in the home.

The worship of household deities was something that the early Christian church fought against—and continued to fight for centuries. Eventually the ancient household deities were, for the most part, relegated to mythology, folk-tales, and fairy tales. In the last few decades, some have made comebacks in role-playing games, modern literature, movies, and video games.

Along with or instead of a general household deity, a domestic witch may choose to select a different patron for each room and/or activity in the house: the master bedroom might be watched over by the Greek Eros, the playful god of sex and amorous desire; the children's rooms looked after by Kwan Yin, whom mothers invoke for the well-being of their children; the laundry room might be governed by Saulé, the Baltic goddess who oversees all spheres of domestic work, including laundering.

While you might already have a god or goddess you work with as a patron deity, having one that can primarily be petitioned for the security and safety of your family, pets, and property might be a welcome addition to your personal pantheon.

A HOUSEHOLD GUARDIAN FOR YOUR HEARTH

Consider adding a guardian statue or spirit house to your hearth or family altar. Different religions and cultures believe that a house, or perhaps the land it sits on, has a ready-made guardian attached to it, and many utilize statues to help focus the protective energy of those guardians. In China, these are fierce-looking guardian lions called *shishi* (sometimes called "foo dogs"). In Japan they are *komainu*. In other cultures, people forgo the statue and erect a "spirit house" instead to provide a resting place for unincarnated guardian spirits. In Scott Cunningham's book *The Magical Household*, he suggests creating a thought-form being who will reside in a statue of your choosing.

Whether you opt to find or create a statue or just build or decorate a small house (you can often find a variety of unpainted wooden birdhouses at craft stores which can be transformed) for your guardian, you first need to get its attention.

During a quiet time at home, sit and meditate on the spirit looking over your household. If your tradition includes casting circles, I'd suggest casting one for this exercise. Speak out loud to the guardian and request that it work with you to watch over your home and all its inhabitants. Ask it to share with you what form it would like to have or what form its shelter should look like. This will hopefully result in your seeing the image in your mind. It might take a few meditation sessions to hone in on something, but stick with it! Once the guardian has shown you what it would like, search for or construct something as close to this as you can.

When you've got just the right representation, place it on or near your hearth, looking out over where your family gathers. Place a small offering bowl beside it, and express to the guardian that the family hopes that it is pleased with your choice. Put small offerings into the bowl each morning or at least once a week. Bits of bread, seeds, or nuts are all good choices.

Keeping the guardian happy is usually a simple matter. Keep his statue or spirit house free of dust. Acknowledge the statue on a regular basis and express your thanks for the guardian's help in keeping you and your family safe. Treat the guardian as an honored family elder. Should you move to another place, make sure to announce to the guardian that you'll be moving and invite him to come along. The statue or spirit house should be one of the first things unpacked in your new home.

DOMESTIC DEITIES

Before choosing and inviting a deity into your home, you'll need to do a bit of research though. While a brownie might seem like a welcome animistic deity to have in your home, anger one and it will go "boggart," transforming into a being that you certainly don't want hanging around! Different deities require different invitations, different care, and different offerings to keep them happy. As always, hit the books before working with any deity.

The following is by no means a complete list of deities you could work with as a domestic witch, nor am I giving every detail about every deity. Consider it a jumping-off point. If you feel called, make sure to take the time to get to know your newfound deity before starting your work with him or her.

Agni (India)

God of fire and lightning, the Hindu deity Agni watches over all. And he doesn't just rule over fire, Agni is the actual embodiment of fire, especially domestic fires. In this form, he already resides in almost every home. His other incarnations include lightning, the sun, and funerary fires. He is pictured as forever young, as he is "relit" every day. Agni is often depicted as a man riding a ram with two heads, faces smeared with butter, and seven tongues. Altars to Agni should be placed in the southwest, as he rules over this direction. Offer

Agni clarified butter and decorate his altar with his symbols, which include any form of fire, rams, parrots, and prayer beads.

Al-Lat (Arabia)

From pre-Islamic Arabia, Al-Lat is a domestic deity whose titles include "Giver of Children" and "Mother of the Gods." Her name literally means "The Goddess." Some consider her the feminine form of Allah, while others call her his daughter. Along with Al Uzza and Menat, Al-Lat forms a trinity of goddesses whose names were banished from post-Islamic holy books. Petition Al-Lat to watch over your home or when you are seeking to become pregnant. Her symbols are the moon, white stones, and silver. Offer Al-Lat fruit, cinnamon, incense, or perfume.

Amaterasu (Japan)

Amaterasu, although not a traditional domestic deity, makes this list because she protects and provides for all who follow her. Create a relationship with this goddess, and you will have her blessings on your home and family. A Japanese Shinto goddess, Amaterasu embodies the sun and her image can be found on the flag of Japan. She grew the first rice in heaven and allowed her grandson to bring it to earth to feed her people. Her sacred day is the winter solstice; offer her rice, silk, or chrysanthemums.

Ancestors

Your own family ancestors are usually very happy to be remembered and asked for their help. And while you might speak directly to a relative whom you know personally that has passed on, you can also call to your generic ancestors, inviting anyone of your bloodline who might hear your plea. Be sure to honor the ancestors that you work with at Samhain, and any time you feel that they have intervened on your behalf. A simple shelf holding photos and mementos of your loved ones makes a perfect ancestor altar. These are usually the easiest type of household guardians to invite into your home and work with.

Annapurna (India)

This food goddess is said to bless a family with an ample supply of sustenance just for the simple act of saying her name first thing in the morning and again at night before you sleep. Ask for Annapurna's blessings as you cook and keep her image in the kitchen or near the dinner table. Be sure when working with her that you do not waste food—that's something this goddess cannot abide. Annapurna is also a goddess of generosity, so sharing your food with others less fortunate will bring her blessings to your home as well. Her symbol is a simple silver vase. As an act of thanks, keep one on your altar and gather spare change in it. When it's full, use the collected money to purchase dry goods to donate to the local food pantry.

Ba Chua Xu (Vietnam)

Also known as "Lady of the Realm," Ba Chua Xu is a Vietnamese goddess who provides not only domestic happiness to her followers, but can also grant fertility and success in both business and education. If you work with Ba Chua Xu, be sure to never give your word if you aren't certain you can keep it; she hands out strict punishment to followers who break their promises. Her most sacred days are those from the 23rd to the 27th of Vietnam's fourth lunar month. Offer Ba Chua Xu incense, wine, tea, or a snippet of your own hair.

Baku (China)

Baku is "The Dream Eater," a protective spirit who devours the nightmares of children and turns them into blessings. Descriptions of Baku vary greatly, but the oldest images usually depict it having the nose of an elephant, the tail of an ox, the body of a bear, and the feet of a tiger. Modern versions often resemble a tapir. To ensure that Baku will watch over your child, simply place a stuffed animal, picture, or even just a painting of his name representing Baku in your child's room. After a bad dream, the child only has to call out "Eat it, Baku!" three times, and Baku will devour the bad dreams and leave his blessings.

Bast (Egypt)

Bast is best known for her association with cats, but she also watches over married couples, children, and women while they are in labor. This makes her a wonderful domestic deity for families, especially those that are young and growing. Petition Bast when doing works associated with sex, fertility, and prosperity. Offerings to Bast include images of cats, catnip, honey, or perfumes. Consider putting a basket near your altar to fill with cat-friendly items. When it's full, donate it to a local shelter in her honor.

Baubo (Greece)

Though Christianity cast her as a demon, Baubo was once known as the liberated, bawdy goddess of humor. She is often depicted showing off her lady parts in the sacred act of ana-suromai (the showing of the vagina) or as an actual walking vagina. Baubo is credited with performing ana-suromai to

lighten the heart of the mourning Demeter as she grieved for the loss of her daughter Persephone. Demeter was so heartened by a good laugh she went on to petition Zeus for his help in releasing Persephone from the clutches of Hades. Baubo looks after women and children and can be petitioned to bring good cheer to your home or laughter into your life after a loss.

Bean-Sidhe (Ireland)

Each family is said to have a bean-sidhe attached to it. This female spirit manifests when she senses that a member of the family is about to pass to the next life. She lets out a loud wail to mourn but also leads him or her on to the afterlife.

Benten (Japan)

Also known as Benzaiten, Daibenzaiten, and Myouonten, Benten is a water goddess sometimes equated with Aphrodite and Sarasvati. She is frequently portrayed sitting on a lotus leaf or riding a dragon. Some images depict her as having eight arms. In her hands she holds the following: a bow, a spear, an arrow, a sword, an axe, a wheel, a pestle, and a length of silk rope. Benten joins the ranks of possible domestic deities since she can be petitioned for help with love, sex, fertility, and good fortune in marriage. Place an egg (a favorite food of snakes) on your altar to honor Benten.

Berchta (Germany)

Berchta, "The Bright One," is from a long line of much beloved goddesses eventually turned demonic by the Christian church. In her original form, Berchta was associated with household affairs. A beautiful woman usually wearing a white dress, she is often accompanied by a goose. In some stories she has one foot significantly larger than the other; called a "swan foot," this deformity was thought to be a sign of someone who could shape-shift. Because of her attributes, Berchta is often thought to have been the basis for the stories of Mother Goose. This goddess looks after all children, but especially those who have passed on. She cares for them in her garden until they are ready to be reincarnated. Berchta also looks after animals and can be petitioned to bless marriages. Honor Berchta at Yule or on January 6 (Twelfth Night), once known as Berchtentag in Germany. Add keys, holly, or representations of geese to your altar to symbolize Berchta. She enjoys an alcoholic drink as an offering, as well.

Bes (Egypt)

A protector of households, Bes looks after everyone in the family, but he has a soft spot for mothers and children. Bes is sometimes depicted as a small man (perhaps a dwarf) with a bushy beard; other times he's shown as a lion on its hind legs. Work with Bes to protect your home and your children or for fertility or sex issues. He can also drive away malevolent spirits. Bes is especially helpful for mothers in labor and will stay by a newborn's side to keep an eye out for trouble. If a baby laughs for no reason, you can be sure that Bes is nearby, entertaining him or her with funny faces. To bring the blessings of Bes to your home, partake in his favorite activities: singing and dancing.

Brighid (Ireland)

Though Brighid wears many hats, one of her oldest is that of patron of the domestic arts. In this guise, she watches over sacred fires, sacred waters, education, and fertility. The domestic witch can turn to Brighid to restore her spirit when she's feeling put upon. Petition her for a reminder that the work you do honors her as well as your family. Pay tribute to Brighid by lighting a candle for her. Leave her offerings of oats, beer, corn, black cherries, or cloves. Be sure to remember her at Imbolc, her most sacred day.

Brownies (Scotland)

Though some think of them as a type of elf, brownies are more a kind of hob, a friendly household spirit. Small, brown, and hairy, brownies are very friendly guardians who take it upon themselves to finish the family's household chores as they sleep. Brownies become very attached to their chosen family, and may pick one person in particular as their favorite. At the same time, they stay quite separate from the members of the household, and prefer never to be addressed directly. Have a job for your brownie? Mention it out loud as if speaking to yourself. Never try to pay your household brownie for services rendered, but instead leave out milk or cream and a baked sweet (cake or cookies) in a place where he will stumble across it. If a brownie gets mad, he may pick up and leave forever—if you are lucky. Rile your brownie up badly enough, and he may go "boggart" instead, moving things about and playing malicious tricks.

Bwbach (Wales)

The bwbach (or female bwbaches) is much like the Scottish brownie in both looks and temperament. The main difference between brownies and bwbachod (plural of bwbach) seems to be that the bwbach is intent on keeping up Pagan traditions. Clergy of a non-Pagan sort entering his household are likely to get a very unwelcome reaction from the bwbach. He is also disdainful of those who do not imbibe in alcohol and likes nothing more than to see a group gathered in his home enjoying a drink and a nice pipe.

Cardea (Italy)

Cardea is said to be a goddess of hinges and thresholds. She can open what is closed, so she can open the way for us to prosperity and good fortune as well. She also has the power to keep doors closed, refusing entry into our homes to evil spirits, negative entities, and illness. Cardea is especially protective of children and can be invoked to protect them by having a twig of her sacred tree, the hawthorn, hung over the thresholds to their rooms. To honor Cardea, keep your doorways and windowsills cleared and clean. Anoint them with a dab of olive oil to request her protection. Consider erecting a small shelf over the outside of your front door where you can leave small offerings, such as a little bowl of milk or flowers, in her honor.

Chantico (Aztec)

Chantico's name means "She Who Dwells in the House." She watches over household fires and is herself the personification of fire. Chantico keeps an eye on those things that her followers hold precious and prevents their theft. She is associated with prosperity and fertility as well as reigning over both pleasure and pain. Keep a potted cactus, her sacred plant, on your altar or near your fireplace to celebrate Chantico.

Chieh Lin (China)

Chieh Lin is the god of marriage and matchmaking who lives on the moon. He is said to pick out those who are destined to be married and ties their feet together with invisible red string. If you think that your string may have come unknotted, petition Chieh Lin to help you find or reconnect with your predestined partner. Chinese marriage ceremonies sometimes include the happy couple drinking out of two stemmed glasses tied together with red string. If you're already attached and want to request Chieh Lin's blessing to your marriage, add two candlesticks holding white or pink candles to your altar, tying them together with red silk thread.

Daikoku (Japan)

Also known as "Lord of the Kitchen," Daikoku is a household guardian who blesses those who follow him with prosperity and success. Keep a statue of Daikoku in the kitchen and rub it to bring luck. Daikoku is often worshipped side by side with the god Ebisu, who is either his son or brother. Together they protect the food stores of those who honor them and answer the prayers of those who tend to domestic affairs. Offer them rice, rice cakes, rice flour, and incense, especially on Kinoene (Elder Rat Day) on or around November 17.

Deives (Lithuania)

Deives are guardian spirits that watch over women who do traditional household work. Men who do not show respect for a woman, or who force her to break one of the deives rules, are sternly punished by them. Two of the most important rules of the deives include that no laundry should be done after sunset and there should be no spinning on Thursdays. Some accounts describe the deives as beautiful blond goddesses; others portray them as old crones.

Domovoi (Russia)

The domovoi has several qualities in common with the Scottish brownie. He's said to be small, furry, and discreet about his presence in the home, though he may wander the house disguised as cat or a mouse. Angering the domovoi can bring on poltergeist-like behavior. Some consider this household guardian spirit to be an ancestral spirit, but regardless of his origins, the domovoi should always be spoken to with the same respect you would show an elder member of the family. They like to be addressed with the title of "sir" or "grandfather." A happy domovoi will keep your property, family, and pets safe. If you've invited a domovoi into your home, give him an area near the stove or a quiet place in the basement as a space for him to rest in. Leave daily offerings of bread and milk or cream for him there. To help ensure your domovoi's good favor, leave an old but clean pair of shoes near the front door for him to use. If you ever move from your home to a new place, make sure to let the domovoi know that you are leaving and invite him to come along.

Dosojin (Japan)

In ancient times, dosojin were spirits who offered protection to travelers. Small stone carvings shaped like humans were placed on roadways to ask the blessings of the dosojin on those who passed by. In more modern times, the dosojin have taken on the care of marriages, fertility, pregnancy, and childbirth. Also known as Sae-no-Kami, the dosojin usually work in pairs. Remember them on January 15, a fire festival on which those who revere the dosojin burn their paper New Year's decorations, asking the spirits to grant them prosperity for the new year.

Duende (Spain and Portugal)

Though duende are considered to be the wandering spirits of unwanted babies in some Latin American countries, most stories describe them as brownie-like hobs. The term *duende* translates to "Master of the House." Duende can be mischievous, but their games are playful and not meant to harm. Unlike most other hob guardian spirits who like to live near the stove, a duende will occupy the space between walls. The sounds that people usually think are the house "settling" are his movements through the house.

Fornax (Rome)

Fornax is a hearth goddess who watches over bread making; her name literally means "oven." Fornax keeps bread from burning and fire from destroying the home. To invite Fornax into your home, give your oven a good scrub and then bake a loaf of bread in it before anything else. If you're short on time, most grocery stores have frozen bread that can be popped right into the oven. Honor Fornax by keeping your oven and the area it occupies clean and tidy. In ancient times, during the festival called Fornacalia, families would hold simple feasts of bread, fruit, and cakes to thank Fornax for her blessings. Fornax can be honored at any time, but her sacred festival falls between February 5 and 17.

Freya (Norse)

Freya is one of the best-loved deities in the world as a goddess of witchcraft, war, and death; yet we often overlook her domestic side. Freya also rules over marriage, fertility, childbirth, and the domestic arts. Her favored people include mothers, soldiers, and those who work magic. As Friday is literally "Freya's Day," be sure to pay tribute to her with offerings of milk, honey, apples, pork, or strawberries. Another way to honor this goddess is to care for cats, one of her sacred animals.

Gabija (Lithuania)

This hearth-fire goddess not only looks after the family's cooking fire, she is the fire. In the modern home, Gabija would take her place in the stove. Gabija's name means "to protect," and she can be invoked to safeguard the home from both thieves and negative energies. To show your respect for this goddess, keep your cooking area clean and give her offerings of a pinch of bread or a sprinkle of salt placed directly into the flames of your cooking fire. Until the early twentieth century, household cooks would make two loaves of bread when baking: a large one for the family and a small one for the goddess. At night a bowl of clean water would be left near the hearth so that Gabija could bathe if she chose to.

Ganesha

Known as "The Remover of Obstacles," Ganesha can be petitioned for love, good sex, luck, and prosperity, among other things. He watches over anyone who cares to pay tribute to him, as long as it is done with sincerity. Ganesha is  a favorite among those who write, and authors often invoke him before starting a book or project. Also known as "Lord of Beginnings," Ganesha can be invoked at the initial phase of any project, new beginning, or travel. Ganesha's immense popularity has grown far past the Hindu faithful, and he is honored in households around the world. Traditional worship of Ganesha includes a simple altar holding his statue at which incense is lit each morning and each evening. A small tray may be added to the altar for his favorite offerings of candy or peanuts. These offerings may be eaten later as "prasad" or "divine food," which brings the god's blessings to those who consume it.

Genius (Rome)

According to Roman mythology, a guardian spirit called a "genius" protects each man. (Women are protected by a juno.) These spirits may be ancestral spirits from the underworld who come to watch over family members for their lifetime. The genius provides protection and helps assure a man's success. You can honor your genius each year on your birthday by giving thanks and offerings at the family altar.

Goblin

While you may consider goblins to be generally troublesome spirits that you would not want to invite into your home, it is possible that one will take up residence without being invited. If you leave the goblin small gifts, you can often win his favor and good behavior. To rid your home of an unwanted goblin whose mischief is becoming too much, strew flaxseeds across the floor of your kitchen several nights in a row. The goblin will feel compelled each night to pick up the flax, seed by seed, keeping him from committing any trickery. After a few nights, he'll be so frustrated that he will move on to another house where he can get back to his dastardly ways unimpeded. A female goblin is usually referred to as a "hag" or "crone."

Grugach (Northern Ireland and the Scottish Highlands)

The grugach are helpful household spirits, much like brownies. They are hard workers who will look after the household and any animals that might be living on the property; they are especially fond of cattle. While the Irish version of the grugach describes them as short, hairy, and usually naked, in the Scottish Highlands they are seen as handsome fairies wearing green clothing. In Scottish traditions, the grugach is thought to be linked to the Green Man. No matter his appearance, never offer a grugach an article of clothing, because to do so is to ask them to leave your home forever.

Hathor (Egypt)

Whole books have been written on Hathor, as one of the oldest known deities of Egypt. She has more forms than can be counted, though her most ancient manifestation is as a cow. Hathor is the personification of nature in that she creates and maintains everything. She embodies the spirit of love, pleasure, and motherhood. She helps women to give birth and the dead to find their way to rebirth; meanwhile she watches over everything in between. Though Hathor will look after anyone who venerates her, among her favorite people are women, aromatherapists, soothsayers, and magical practitioners. Be sure to include images of cows on her altar and to provide one of her most favored offerings: beer.

Heinzelmännchen (Germany)

The *heinzelmännchen* (Hine-tzel-men-shen) is a house gnome. While the inhabitants of the household sleep, the heinzelmännchen finishes up any chores that were not completed during the day. Heinzelmännchen who feel that they are being taken advantage of by lazy folks leaving chores undone on purpose will leave the household forever.

Hera (Greece)

Though some stories depict Hera as the put-upon shrew and jealous wife of cheating Zeus, she was widely worshipped long before being paired with him. Called "Lady of the Beasts," Hera was a sacred cow goddess called upon for fertility and abundance. After wedding Zeus, her role became more that of mother and wife. Hera can be petitioned for virtually any need, but she is a popular goddess to invoke to bless handfasting and weddings or to watch over childbirth. Women who are feeling weak or in need of strength can ask Hera to empower them with her strength. Offerings to Hera include apples, poppy seeds, honey, and incense.

Hestia (Greece)

Hestia, goddess of hearth and home, has an ever-growing following among those who find domestic life sacred. Watching over domestic duties, family, home life, and security, Hestia chose to dedicate herself to the service of others and to her community. In ancient Greece, hearth fires were kept constantly burning in Hestia's honor; rituals were required to either put out or light the fire. Hestia herself kept the hearth fires burning on Mt. Olympus. Hestia can be invoked by the simple lighting of a candle or stove while saying, "I honor you, Hestia, as I light this flame." It is also traditional to give Hestia the first and last bite of every meal. Keeping a small offering bowl and a red candle in your kitchen creates a simple altar to Hestia. Before partaking of a meal, put a pinch in the bowl, and repeat this when clearing the dishes. The offering can later be disposed of or put outside.

Isis (Egypt)

Also called Auset, Isis is perhaps the most venerated of all goddesses on earth. She is the Universal Mother Goddess, a moon goddess who watches over those who follow her, though she has a soft spot for women, mothers, and magical practitioners. A faithful and loving goddess, Isis also possesses immense power and wisdom. Stories from myth state that Isis got her ability to heal and to practice magic after tricking Ra into revealing his secret name to her, therefore giving Isis the ability to call on his divine powers. Honor Isis by wearing her symbol, the ankh, playing the sistrum (an ancient Egyptian musical instrument), or offering her honey, milk, or incense at her altar.

Ix Chebel Yax (Maya)

This goddess, whose home is on the moon, watches over all the details of home life. She is also known as Ix U Sihnal or "Moon Patroness of Birth." Under this latter guise she watches over conception and answers prayers for live births. Ix Chebel Yax is also credited for teaching humans the arts of spinning and weaving. Her images often portray her as wearing a headdress containing a spindle of cotton thread.

Juno (Goddess, Rome)

Associated with the Greek goddess Hera, Juno is "The Great Goddess" who watches over women, marriages, and children. She is sometimes referred to as "She Who Gives," a title conferred because of her willingness to grant prosperity and fertility to those of her followers who ask for it. This goddess also oversees the reproductive cycles of women — from first cycle, through pregnancy, and into menopause. Juno can be honored on the first day of every month with offerings of figs, wine, or flowers.

Juno (Guardian, Rome)

According to Roman mythology, just as every man is protected by a genius, each woman has a juno who looks out for her throughout her life, focusing specifically on marriage and childbirth. Thought to be an ancestral spirit, you can honor your juno at each birthday with offerings at the family altar.

Kamui Fuchi (Japan)

Kamui Fuchi is a hearth goddess who not only watches over the hearth, she lives in it! To invite Kamui Fuchi into your home, give your oven a good scrubbing and make sure to keep it clean. Those who neglect their hearth fire will be subject to her displeasure. Keeping on her good side ensures good relations with spirits in general, and specifically with your ancestral spirits, since the hearth is said to be a gateway to the spirit world and Kamui Fuchi is a gatekeeper. Leave this goddess small bowls of cooked rice as an offering. She should also always be given the first sip of any beer you partake in.

Kane (Hawaii)

A creator god, Kane (Kah-nay) was worshipped as an ancestor of both chiefs and common people. His name translates to "husband." Kane created heaven for the gods; the "lower heaven" positioned above the earth where he placed the sun, moon, and stars; and the earth which he filled with plants, animals, and humans. He then assigned the other gods their domains to rule. Kane is a kind god and, when called upon, will give his blessings to all who live in a household. A traditional offering to Kane is sugarcane, but the modern worshipper could easily substitute raw sugar.

Kikimora (Russia)

In Russia every household is said to have a kikimora, a type of female house spirit. Sometimes described as the wife of the male guardian spirit, the domovoi, the kikimora helps with the housework and the care of any animals that might live on the property. But if those living in the home leave too much of their work for the kikimora, she will get back at them by tickling them or whistling in their ears while they try to sleep. The only way to win her favor back is to brew a huge tub of fern tea and wash all the household pots and pans in it. She likes to live behind the stove or in the basement or cellar. Seeing a kikimora spinning or doing needlework was a sign of the impending death of someone in the household.

Kishimo-Jin (Japan)

Once a child-eating demon, Kishimo-Jin was saved from her cannibalism when Buddha gave her pomegranates to feed on instead. She converted to Buddhism and became a deity for women in childbirth and a protector of children. Offer her pomegranates or peaches in exchange for her keeping an eye on your children.

Kobold (Germany)

The kobold is a form of hobgoblin whose history goes back at least as far as the thirteenth century. According to some tales, every home has a kobold. There are some kobolds that manifest as fire and live in the family's hearth; these are referred to as drakes. Like the brownie, during the night he will help with unfinished chores around the house, and he will turn mischievous if mistreated. Unlike the brownie, the kobold loves gifts. If you share your home with a kobold, leave him a small portion of the family's dinner each night at the same time and in the same place. A well-treated kobold brings their family luck and prosperity.

Lares (Rome)

In ancient Rome, lares were guardian spirits connected to a particular area: a piece of property, a roadway, a town, or a state might have its own lar (singular of lares). If a household were under the protection of a lar, that service would be based on them living on property that the lar watched over, distinguishing them from the Roman penates, guardians of a particular family that would move with them wherever they lived. Lares and penates were often honored together at the family shrine, usually alongside the goddess Vesta. Offer the lares of your property wheat breads, grapes, incense, or wine.

Mama Occlo (Inca)

Mama Occlo's name means "Mother Fertility"; she can grant children to her followers who petition her. A goddess of domestic arts, Mama Occlo, daughter of Mama Quilla, taught humans how to spin and weave. As a mother goddess, she brings feelings of warmth to the homes of her followers and protects them.

Mama Quilla (Inca)

This moon deity, whose name translates to "Mother Moon," is a goddess of marriage and protector of women and children. She is considered to be the mother of the whole Incan race. Mama Quilla is also responsible for the changing of the seasons and the flow of time. Her tears hitting the earth generated the metal silver. Represent her on your altar with images of the moon, especially those made of silver.

Minerva (Rome)

Though Minerva might well be known more in her guise as a goddess of wisdom, she is also a patroness of household tasks. Honor Minerva while going about your daily chores. Minerva can also be worked with for healing, music, and any arts or crafts. Invoke Minerva when you're creating—alone or with your children—by lighting a yellow candle.

Nisse (Norway, Denmark)

A nisse (plural nisser) is a household spirit that cares for a farm. In some Scandinavian countries, belief in the nisser lasted until well into the nineteenth century. Nisser are said to carry out many different kinds of farming tasks from tending to the horses to carrying bales of hay. A nisse requires the respect of those he shares a home with and a daily offering of porridge with butter.

Penates (Rome)

Penates are Roman household deities, sometimes considered to be ancestral spirits. Once considered gods of the pantry or food stores, they eventually became guardians of the whole house. In ancient times, every Roman dwelling held a household shrine where statues or cloth poppets of the penates resided. The penates took part in every aspect of household life and helped guard and provide for their family. In turn, families would set out plates of food for the penates, or they would throw their food offering into the hearth fire. These household guardians are easily confused with lares. Lares, however, are connected with the land, and will protect a family based on them living on that land. Penates are bound to those living in the home and would travel with them if the family were to move to a new domain. Lares and penates were often honored together at the family shrine, usually alongside the goddess Vesta.

Piskies (Cornwall)

Mischievous but helpful, piskies are somewhat similar to brownies or the nisser of farms. They will do chores around the house at night for a respectful family, but when they feel dishonored, watch out! There are a few famous individual piskies, including Coleman Grey who would trade places with abused children and wreak havoc on their parents. When he had decided that the parents had learned their lesson, he would return the changeling. Probably the most popular of all piskies is Joan the Wad, queen of the piskies, along with her consort Jack O'Lantern. Carrying or housing an image of Joan is said to bring luck and happiness.

Saulé (Lithuania)

Goddess of the domestic arts and of the sun, Saulé rules over hearth fires, spinning, weaving, and fertility. A very independent goddess, she is particularly fond of single mothers. If the offerings left are to her liking, Saulé has been known to help women with their laundry. Saulé is, in addition, a sun goddess; she spins rays of sunlight on her wheel. Good offerings for this goddess include flowers, fresh vegetables, and apples.

Teraphim (Hebrew)

Teraphim is a Hebrew word for household gods similar to lares and penates, embodied in small, human-shaped statues that were kept in a family's house or carried by nomadic tribes. These statues were worshipped as divine objects and were said to bring good luck, comfort, and prosperity. Teraphim were accepted in Christian worship early on and mentioned in the Old Testament. Later they were condemned, and the term became known to mean "disgraceful things."

Vesta (Rome)

Vesta is a goddess of domestic fires. While she is considered to be the equivalent of the Greek goddess Hestia, Vesta's role in Roman life was much more significant. She was worshipped in every Roman household, and while she often shared shrines with lares and penates, she was always the first deity honored. Offerings to Vesta were often a portion of the family's meal, thrown directly into the hearth fire. Honor her in your own home by throwing a pinch of bread into the fire of your stovetop.

Zao Jun (China)

This domestic god from China protects the home and family and cares for both the physical and emotional needs of those who honor him. His place is by the hearth, so modern-day followers hang his paper image over the stove. One of

Zao Jun's responsibilities is to watch over the happenings of the home and report them back to the Jade Emperor on the 23rd day of the last lunar month. The Jade Emperor deals out rewards or punishments based on these reports. Thankfully, if a family has not been perfect, they can sway Zao Jun into a better report by holding a feast called "Xiao Nian" before New Year's. During this feast, incense is burned and Zao Jun's favorite foods are served. To ensure his words to the emperor are sweet, honey is smeared across the mouth of his image over the stove. On New Year's day, "Xiao Nianay," the image is burned to speed Zao Jun on his trip to the Jade Emperor, and a new image is placed above the oven.

four

Magical Recipes

The easiest way to add magic to your day is to infuse your cooking with it. If you don't already, start taking advantage of the natural magical properties of foods. By being conscious of your ingredients and their attributes, you can create meals full of your intent.

Start off by getting to know the properties of foods you use on a regular basis. As you add them to your recipes, concentrate on your intent. Want to create a meal that will have your lover eager to get to "dessert"? Plan it around foods that inspire desire. As you add each ingredient, state your intent. For example, "I add this ginger for lusty thoughts!"

Always stir clockwise when dealing with recipes that will add to something or grow something, such as buckwheat pancakes for prosperity. If you are whipping up a recipe to get rid of something instead, such as a bad habit, stir counterclockwise.

You can create a myriad of recipes of all sorts using the magical herbal correspondences in chapter 5. But first let me share with you a few of my own personal magical recipes, using everyday herbs, spices, and foods to whip up herbal blends, simmering incense, magical oils, house washes and floor sweeps, and other magical concoctions.

They are all designed to be quick and convenient, and rely on the traditional uses of herbs. Don't forget to infuse each recipe with your own personal intentions—following the instructions alone will not get the magic flowing! Mix and match ingredients, use herbal mixes as incense instead of making up an oil, or take the herbs from an herbal blend and create an oil. Write a chant to say while you're mixing. Creating magical potions and notions is an intuitive process where you can really dive in and make something special!

HERBAL BLENDS

You can grind dried herbs together into a powder to burn over self-lighting charcoal as incense, throw directly into your grill after you've finished cooking, or sprinkle right over your lit stove (always do so very carefully using a small pinch and away from children and pets). Herbal blends can also be used to roll candles in, to cast circles when working on specific needs, or to enhance a mojo or charm bag. Add herbs to a pot of water and bring to a low boil to create a simmering potpourri. For these recipes, combine the ingredients and grind well in a mortar and pestle or an old coffee grinder. Store any extra in a tightly sealed container away from light and heat.

Communication Blend

Whether you need to give a speech, make a convincing argument, or produce a written work, this blend can help you find the right words.

- 1 part caraway seeds
- 1 part thyme
- ¼ part cinnamon
- Beans from one vanilla pod

Creativity Mix

Dress a yellow candle with avocado oil and roll it in this mix, then burn the candle while enjoying creative endeavors. If you're creating something for sale, dress the candle in grapeseed oil instead. You can sprinkle a small amount of this herbal combination in with any artistic or craft supplies to help bolster your creativity when using them.

- 2 parts instant coffee granules
- 2 parts cinnamon
- 1 part dried grapefruit peel

Divination Mix

Sprinkle this mix into the bag or box that holds your tarot cards, runes, or other divination tools. You can also dress a candle with grapeseed oil, and then roll it in this mix of herbs to burn while doing a reading, or throw it directly into your scrying fire.

- 1 part bay leaf
- 1 part nutmeg
- 1 part thyme
- 1 whole star anise (increase for larger batches)

Friendship Mix

Burn as an incense or set out as potpourri while entertaining friends to strengthen your bonds and facilitate lively conversation.

- 4 parts dried orange or clementine peel
- 2 parts clove
- 1 part thyme

Happy Family Blend

This blend is a perfect mix to burn or leave out as a potpourri. It inspires feelings of peace and happiness.

- 1 part allspice
- 1 part cloves
- 1 part nutmeg
- 1 part ground, dried orange or clementine peel
- ½ part cinnamon
- Contents of a chamomile tea bag

Love Blend

Dust a fine powder of this mix on your clothes or your hands before spending time with your partner to strengthen loving bonds.

- 4 parts dried apple peel
- 4 parts red rose petals
- 2 parts cocoa powder
- 1 part cinnamon

To give the above mix a lustier vibe, substitute coriander for the rose petals and add 2 parts ginger.

Make a Wish! Mix

Be sure to grind finely. Throw a pinch of this mix into a fire and make a wish!

- 2 parts ground bay leaf
- 2 parts cinnamon
- 2 parts star anise
- 1 part ginger

Protection Mix

Burn this around your home when you feel physically or psychically threatened. I mix up a large batch of this twice a year and sprinkle it all around the outside of my house. A pinch or two in your children's shoes when they leave the house couldn't hurt either!

- 2 parts ginger
- 2 parts garlic
- 2 parts cinnamon
- 2 parts cloves
- 2 parts flaxseed
- 2 parts anise seed
- 1 part dill
- 1 part black pepper

Spirit Away Mix

Produce a large batch to sprinkle around the borders of your property or around your home to keep unwanted spirits out. Always burn before moving into a new house. This mix is wonderful to carry with you to graveyards; sprinkle it behind you, across your path, to help ensure you're not followed home.

- 4 parts fennel seed
- 4 parts dill weed
- 4 parts rosemary
- 2 parts basil
- 1 part salt

Study Blend

Burn while reviewing for a big test.

- 2 parts rosemary
- ½ part clove
- Contents of one Earl Grey tea bag

SIMMERING INCENSE

To create a simmering incense, start off with a pan made of cast iron, copper, or glass. Fill it three-quarters full of clean, cool water, and put it over a medium heat. While that water is warming, mix your ingredients into a bowl one by one. Consider what action you are hoping to generate with this mixture and what each ingredient brings to the recipe. When all the ingredients have been added, stir them together with your hands and say out loud your wishes for the mix. You can do this by coming up with a rhyme, using the words provided here, or by just simply stating your intent.

Pour the mixed herbs into the warming water, turn the heat down to low, and give it all a stir. If you're trying to add something to your home with your magical mix, stir clockwise. Wanting to rid it of a negative feeling? Stir counterclockwise. Let the water simmer and fill your home with the aroma of the mixed herbs and with the magic that they bring. Always keep an eye on the pan so that it doesn't boil dry.

Note: Any of these herb mixes may also be ground together and burned over a self-lighting charcoal tablet. Just make sure to use dried herbs instead of fresh.

Cleansing/Purification Mix

This is a great incense to throw on the stove while you are giving the house a good scrubbing or when there are negative feelings or illnesses bubbling around your home. Throw the windows open and let this mix help clear out all the "ick" from the house. Add half a cup salt, nine whole cloves, one chamomile tea bag, a pinch of peppermint, and a peel and juice of one lemon to a pan of water. Simmer on the stove, stirring counterclockwise. Repeat occasionally, "Salt and herbs please clear this home, no negativity (or illness) now will roam!"

When you are finished cleaning, allow the mix to cool to room temperature, then deposit the contents of your pan on your compost pile; alternately, strain the liquid out and flush it down the commode while throwing the solids away in your outside garbage can.

Kyphi

Kyphi is an ancient Egyptian brew. Its aroma is said to invite benevolent, helpful spirits to your home. Simmer this mix on the stove to cleanse the house and banish negativity. Drinking kyphi is said to cleanse the body, bring on restful sleep, and assure vivid dreams.

Though no specific recipe survives today, what we have here contains all those things that seem to be required. Substitute all water in your pan for half a bottle of red wine. Add a quarter cup of honey, a handful of raisins, and two cinnamon sticks.

Money Draw Mix

When you are trying to increase the cash flow into your life, this money draw brew is just the thing. Over a low heat, add a splash of molasses (about a tablespoon), the rind and juice of an orange, and a knob of fresh ginger (or about a teaspoon of dried) to a pan of water. With a wooden spoon, stir three times clockwise, and then trace a dollar sign on the bottom of the pan with your spoon while saying, "Money, money come to me, quick as lightning. So mote it be!"

Mood Lifting Mix

Feeling a bit blue and just can't shake it off? Try this blend for a little boost of happiness. To your pan of water add one chamomile tea bag, one cinnamon stick, and a healthy pinch of both peppermint and marjoram. If you have any St. John's wort capsules, open one up and add its contents to the mix as well. Give it a stir and say, "Herbs of joy and herbs of play, lift my mood, bring joy today."

Peaceful Family Mix

Start this mix by replacing half the water in your pan with apple juice. Add one chamomile tea bag, several slices of fresh or dried apple, a pinch of sage, and about a tablespoon of dried rice. Stir occasionally while saying, "Tiny herbs of calm and love, bring our home blessings from above."

Romantic Evening Mix

It might not happen as often as we'd like for it to, but when you find yourself and your partner at home alone and want to create just the right mood, simmer up this love and lust booster!

Fill your pan with water and add a healthy splash of red wine. To this mix add equal parts cardamom, coriander seeds, caraway seeds, dried ginger, and cocoa powder. Add a slice of apple peel, a pinch of cayenne, a pinch of paprika, and a few whole cloves. Bring it all to a rolling boil; then reduce the heat to a slow simmer. Say as you stir, "Fiery herbs, three times three, alight a spark for (your partner's name) and me."

Study Mix

When you need to concentrate on learning or memorizing something or before a big test, give this mix a whirl. Into your pan of water add equal parts rosemary, instant coffee crystals, and sage. Take a study break every fifteen or twenty minutes to check the pan and give it a stir. Each time say, "For remembrance and wisdom I stir this brew, let me remember all that I view."

MAGICAL OILS

Magical oils with their wide range of uses are wonderful to have on hand. The simplest way to create a magical oil is to place a layer of herbs in the bottom of a clean glass jar and cover with the oil of your choice (see appendix I for oil correspondences). Cap with a nonmetallic lid or plastic wrap and let it sit for at least a week or as long as a month. Strain the oil well through cheesecloth or a coffee filter into a clean jar. Use it to dress candles or anoint charm bags, appliances, money, bills—anything you need to work a little magic on! Alternately, add the herbs and oil to a small Crock-Pot, set it to warm, and let it brew for five to six hours. Strain and bottle the oil in a clean glass jar with a lid. The shelf life of magical oils will depend greatly on how well they are strained and what type of oil is used. To extend the life of your magical oil, use a mix of 90 percent of your chosen carrier oil and 10 percent jojoba oil.

Attraction Oil

Anoint your pulse points with this oil before you go out to attract the attention of the opposite sex or to get your partner's attention. Dress a red candle with this oil to burn during a romantic evening.

- 1 part red rose petals
- ½ part basil
- Contents of a peppermint tea bag
- Sweet almond oil to cover

Bad Habit Breaking Oil

Need a little something to shore you up while you work on breaking a bad habit? Mix a batch of this oil. Inhale its scent when you feel tempted, or dress a black candle with it to burn when temptation strikes.

- 1 part anise seed
- Contents of an Earl Grey tea bag
- 1/4 part black pepper
- 1/4 part dried ginger or a small knob of fresh, peeled ginger
- Olive oil to cover

Banishing Oil

This powerful oil can be used to dress a black candle when you need to separate yourself from something or someone harmful in your life.

- 2 parts cinnamon
- 2 parts black pepper
- 2 parts cumin
- 1 part cayenne pepper
- Castor oil to cover

Business Success Oil

Use this oil to anoint business cards, your work area, a cash register, a green candle to burn while you work, or the front door of your business.

- 1 part basil
- Contents of one Earl Grey tea bag
- ¼ part ground cinnamon
- Olive oil to cover

Employment Oil

Place just a small dab of this oil on envelopes when sending out your résumé. Rub a bit into your hands before an interview and then make sure to shake hands!

- 1 part ground bay leaf
- 1 part ground coriander
- 1 whole raw (unshelled) pecan
- Sesame oil to cover

Fast Luck Oil

Fast Luck Oil brings good luck your way when used alone. Or add it to a spell to make it work more quickly.

- 4 parts ground bay leaf
- 4 parts marjoram
- 1 part ground cinnamon
- Peanut oil to cover

Fire Oil

Fire oil helps ignite passion or desire, increases bravery, or can spark action in someone who is procrastinating. Use it to anoint a red candle to burn while you're with your partner, anoint court papers to help get a faster decision, or rub a small amount on your hands to help bolster your confidence—and get your audience excited—before a speech. If possible, make this oil on Sunday.

- 1-inch strip of orange peel or 1 part dried, ground peel
- 3 parts cinnamon
- 1 part clove
- 1 part nutmeg
- Sesame oil to cover

Prosperity Oil

Use prosperity oil in place of Business Success Oil if you're particularly looking for monetary success in business. Also use it to anoint your bank statements, wallet or purse, your piggy bank, or a green candle to burn while you do prosperity work. Anoint a dollar bill before putting it in a charity container; by sharing what you have, it's sure to come back to you! Create this oil on a Thursday to maximize its effectiveness.

- 1 part alfalfa (check the pet aisle where rabbit food is sold)
- Contents of a chamomile tea bag (increase for larger batches)
- 1 part coriander
- Corn oil to cover
- 1 penny or small magnet (optional)

Reversing Oil

Use this oil when you want to protect yourself against negativity or psychic attack and send that nasty energy back to its source.

- 1-inch strip of fresh lemon peel or 1 part dried, ground peel
- 1 part rosemary
- Contents of a peppermint tea bag (increase to 2 bags for larger mixes)
- Corn oil to cover

Visions Oil

This magical oil can be used to anoint candles to burn while practicing divination. Dab a tiny bit on your "third eye" to help increase your psychic awareness or before bed to induce prophetic dreams.

- 1- inch strip of fresh lemon peel or 1 part dried, ground peel
- 2 parts ground bay leaf
- 1 part nutmeg
- 1 part thyme
- Cover with grapeseed oil

HERBAL HOUSE WASH

There are several ways to create a magical floor wash. The simplest is to place herbs that correspond to what you are trying to achieve in a bowl. Pour hot water over the herbs and let them steep for ten to fifteen minutes; drain the liquid into a bucket and add warm tap water and the cleaning product of your choice. Castile soap or cleaning products made with pine oil are both good choices. As the solids you've strained away haven't been affected by the act of cleansing, they can either be composted or just thrown away. Use the mix to clean floors, walls, door frames, and windowsills. Always be careful to use lightly colored herbs to avoid staining. You can use an herbal wash to cleanse your house of negative energies or to promote positive feelings, such as love or calm. When doing the actual cleansing, wash clockwise when drawing things to you, counterclockwise when ridding your home of unwanted energies.

If you leave out the cleaning product, these infusions can also be added to a ritual bath to impart the same properties directly to you. Allow one cup of infused wash for a tub three-quarters full of water. If utilizing as an herbal bath, be sure to close your eyes tightly and dunk your head under the water a time or two.

Four Thieves Wash

Use this wash to repel illness and for protection.

- 1 part rosemary
- 1 part black salt
- A splash of Four Thieves Vinegar

Good Luck Wash

Need something to help turn things around for your family? Try a good house scrubbing that includes this blend.

- 2 chamomile tea bags
- 1 part marjoram
- 1 part oregano
- A handful of peanut shells

Happy Marriage Mix

Use this wash after an argument to heal feelings and reconnect. It's also a great blend to use on anniversaries or days that are special to you and your partner to create a loving, happy mood.

- 1 part marjoram
- 1 part dried apple peel
- 1 whole star anise
- ½ part fennel seed
- 1 chamomile tea bag

Health and Healing Wash

Whether you are trying to fend off that flu that is going around or you are about to conduct a healing ritual for a family member or pet, give the house a quick wipe down with this herbal wash.

- 2 parts sage
- 2 parts thyme

- 2 parts rosemary
- 1 part salt
- 1 part dill
- A handful of shredded, unsweetened coconut
- A handful of pine needles (if available)

Heartbreak Ease Wash

If your family has suffered a loss and you're looking for something to ease the pain and start the healing process, this wash might be just the start.

- 1 part fennel seed
- 1 part marjoram
- 1 part fresh or dried chives
- A handful of raw almonds

Protection Wash

This floor wash includes ingredients meant to help cleanse and purify your home and promote peaceful, happy feelings. Throw open your windows while you wash down the house with this blend, and finish up by burning the Happy Family herbal blend over self-lighting charcoal blocks or by creating kyphi as a simmering incense.

- 2 parts rosemary
- 2 parts basil
- 2 large bay leaves
- 2 parts ginger
- 2 parts sea salt
- 1 part dried garlic
- 1 part black pepper

Stress Management

Every family goes through its stressful times, whether from financial, relationship, or any of the myriad other troubles that a household can find themselves in. A thorough wash down with this blend can ease tempers and relieve anxiety.

- 2 chamomile tea bags
- 1 part culinary sage
- 1 part fennel seed
- ½ part salt
- ½ part ground cloves

After straining the herbs and adding the liquid to your cleaning bucket, pour in half a can of your favorite brand of beer along with the water and cleanser.

Successful Business Wash

To help promote more successful business opportunities, use this wash in your business or to wipe down your personal work space. To be less conspicuous at work, blend this at home, but leave out the cleanser. Soak a clean cloth in the wash, wring it out slightly, and place it in a sealable plastic bag or container and carry it to work. Use the cloth to quickly wipe down your workstation or desk.

- 2 parts basil
- 2 parts culinary sage
- 1 part mint
- A splash of champagne vinegar (substitute with white vinegar in a pinch)

FLOOR SWEEPS

Floor sweeps can also be used to fill your living or work space with specific intentions or to rid that space of unwanted energies. Gather your choice of herbs corresponding with your intent; depending on the size of the area you are going to sweep, about a quarter cup of mixed herbs is more than enough. Mix the herbs with a base of baking soda (best for cleansing, banishing, or hex breaking) or cornstarch or cornmeal (best for prosperity). If possible, sprinkle the mix around the floor and leave it overnight.

The act of sweeping itself is important to this type of spell. Drawing something to you? Start at your front door and sweep in toward the center of your home. Gather the sweep-up and dispose of it in a respectful way, such as adding it to your compost pile or burying it near your front door. Trying to rid your home of negativity? Sweep counterclockwise through the house and straight out the front door! Gather this sweep in a plain brown bag and carry it off your property. Leave it in a public trash can or pour it out at a crossroads that you don't often travel past. Dispose of the bag in a public trash can away from your property. If you use a vacuum to clean up the sweep, empty the canister or replace the bag immediately and dispose of the contents as outlined above.

Cleansing Sweep

This sweep is not only good for the spiritual energy of an area, its baking soda base will also deodorize any carpets you sprinkle it on! Use it on any carpets at the same time you use the cleansing wash on uncarpeted floors and walls.

- 1 part ground bay leaves
- 1 part dried, ground ginger
- 1 part rosemary
- 1 part dried lemon rind
- Baking soda base

Money Draw Sweep

When you need a little extra cash to cover your expenses, and you've tried everything else to no avail, try a money draw sweep and watch for unusual opportunities.

- 1 part allspice
- 1 part cinnamon
- 1 part nutmeg
- Cornmeal base

Nightmare Prevention Sweep

If someone in the family is having recurring nightmares, sprinkle this sweep in their room before bed. In the morning sweep it up counterclockwise, and dispose of it away from your home.

- 2 parts rosemary
- 2 parts sesame seeds
- 2 parts thyme
- 1 part basil
- Baking soda base

Psychic Dream Sweep

Similar to the nightmare prevention blend, this sweep encourages psychic or prophetic dreams when sprinkled in your room. In the morning, sweep it up clockwise and dispose of it in your compost bin or trash.

- 1 part nutmeg
- 1 part anise seed
- 1 whole star anise
- Contents of a peppermint tea bag
- Soy flour base (if unavailable, substitute with baking soda)

MISCELLANEOUS MAGICAL CONCOCTIONS

The following are a few recipes for various magical concoctions that I've come across over the years. Most fall under the heading of "hoodoo," a form of traditional folk magic.

Ancestor Water

Place a bottle of water on the grave of a relative. Allow it to sit for at least twenty-four hours or as long as a moon cycle. Pour a small amount of this water into a bowl to place on your ancestor altar, especially during the Samhain season or any time you work with your ancestors.

Black Salt

Sometimes called Sal Negro, Witches' Salt, or Drive Away Salt, black salt can be used to drive away evil or negative energies and for protection. Sprinkle it in the doorways and corners of a room or business to dispel negativity or as a safeguard against an unfriendly neighbor or coworker. Make a large batch to sprinkle around your property or gardens for protection. Black salt creates an incredibly strong circle of protection.

There are many different recipes for making black salt, including just dyeing salt black. I've found this recipe to be the strongest for my personal use.

Burn herbs that correspond with protection over a self-lighting charcoal block in a clean cast-iron cauldron or other cast-iron container. If you are making a larger batch, do this several times, removing the completely cooled ash matter to another container between burnings, but not cleaning out the cauldron. When you have what you feel to be enough burned matter, take an old spoon and scrape the cauldron of any sticking ash. Give it a good, hard scrape, as this will add a bit of cast iron to your mix. Add this and your herbal ash to a mortar and pestle or an old coffee grinder, and grind the mix well. To this, add twice as much salt and stir to combine. Store in a tightly covered, labeled jar until ready to use.

Four Thieves Vinegar

Herbal vinegar use is documented back to the time of Hippocrates. Four Thieves Vinegar is said to stem from the time of the black plague. It is traditionally applied to ward off illness and psychic attacks. Sprinkle it outside your home for protection, use it for a salad dressing, or mix it into marinades for meats.

- 16-ounce bottle of vinegar of your choice (I recommend apple cider vinegar, but you can also use white vinegar or red wine vinegar.)
- 1 head of garlic, cloves removed, peeled, and crushed
- 2 tablespoons rosemary
- 1 tablespoon cooking sage
- 1-inch strip of lemon peel

Mix all ingredients together in a jar with a lid. Allow to sit for four to six weeks, shaking daily. Strain into a clean bottle with a tightly fitting lid. Store away from light and heat.

Jupiter Water

Also known as Thunder Water, this is simply rainwater collected during a thunderstorm. Keep it in a well-sealed, labeled bottle. Use Jupiter Water when doing magical workings to send negative energy back to its source or when doing healing magic.

Peace Powder

Use this powder around your house to break hexes or jinxes. It can also be sprinkled inside your home to calm angry feelings and help heal arguments. If there are negative feelings between you and a family member or coworker, sprinkle a pinch of this in their chair, or in an area where they are sure to walk. Mix equal parts rosemary, cumin seed, and basil. To this blend, add an equal part baking soda.

Red Brick Dust

Red brick is used in hoodoo magic for protection and to repel negative energies. Nothing could be simpler to create. All you need is a red brick, a paper sack, and a hammer. Place the brick in the paper sack and strike it until it's a fine dust. Give your front walkway or steps a good scrub. When the area is completely dry, sprinkle the red dust across the threshold. This should be redone about once a week.

five

The Domestic Witch's Herbal

Though I love having more exotic herbs on hand, it's a relief to know that everything I really need is already stocked in my kitchen. The following herbal contains items you can find in your fridge, spice cabinet, or at the local grocery store. Not only does it contain the basic correspondences, but also a few culinary tips and a magical tip or two.

ALFALFA

Alfalfa may not be something you have stocked in your kitchen cabinet already, but it's generally easy to find it in its dried form in the small pet section of your local grocery or pet store.

Form: sprouts, dried

Ruler: Venus

Element: Earth

God: Ogun

Goddesses: Áine, Demeter, Venus

Attributes: employment, love, prosperity

Culinary uses: Fresh alfalfa sprouts can go in green salads, on sandwiches, or with other veggies when making juice.

Magical uses: Place alfalfa in a green bag and hang it in your kitchen to ensure that your cupboards are never bare. Carry it in a mojo bag along with a bay leaf and a pecan when seeking new employment. Ingest alfalfa before asking for a raise to give a boost to your personal income potential.

ALLSPICE

Always buy allspice in its whole form whenever you can. Grinding them fresh gives them a much longer shelf life, and they are also much more aromatic.

Form: dried whole berries or ground

Ruler: Jupiter

Element: Air

Gods: Ellegua, Shango

Goddesses: Ochun, Yemaya

Attributes: business success, employment, healing, luck, money draw, new employment, unblocking

Culinary uses: Allspice flavors Caribbean or Middle Eastern cuisine, apples, chicken, spiced tea, chocolate, curries, pumpkins, cookies, jerk seasoning, spiced rum, seafood, stews, sausages, or pickles.

Magical uses: Add allspice to a mojo bag when you need to succeed or stand out in a crowd, such as at auditions or job interviews. Add to floor sweeps for business success or add a pinch to your shoes before you go out with your child to sell popcorn, cookies, or other goodies for fund-raisers.

ALMOND

Ever wonder why almonds are traditional favors at weddings? The Romans used to shower newlyweds with almonds to bless them with fertility. Add a pinch of almond flour to fertility spells to harness that power for yourself.

Form: extract, flour, oil, nut, paste, marzipan, milk

Ruler: Mercury

Element: Air

Gods: Adonis, Attis, Chandra, Hermes, Jupiter, Liber Pater, Mercury, Obatala, Odin, Oko, Ptah, Thoth, Zeus

Goddesses: Artemis, Athena, Diana, Hecate, Nana, Ochun, Rhea, Yemaya

Attributes: anger management, breaking bad habits, emotional healing (helps mend broken hearts), fertility, love, prosperity (especially in oil form)

Culinary uses: Eat whole as a snack or flavor cookies, ice cream, chocolate, salads, or green beans with almonds or almond derivatives. Grind as a coating for chicken.

Magical uses: Almond oil makes a great base for prosperity oils. Use a piece of light blue cloth to create a mojo bag including three almonds and equal parts powdered clove and marjoram. Carry to ease a broken heart. While trying to stop smoking or improve your eating habits, mindfully eat a few almonds when you get the urge to light up or consume something unhealthy. Pick a mantra to repeat before eating them, such as "I am strong and can break this unhealthy bad habit." Anoint or consecrate objects associated with the element of Air with almond oil.

ALOE VERA

Having an aloe vera plant in your kitchen is said to fend off burns. It's also a very easy plant to grow in a kitchen windowsill. Some larger grocery stores carry large cut leaves in the produce aisle. You can often find aloe gel near the suntan lotion, or aloe juice in the local health-food store.

Form: plant, lotion, juice, gel

Ruler: Moon

Element: Water

Gods: Aeacus, Amun-Ra, Chandra, Indra, Minos, Rhadamanthus, Vulcan

Goddess: Artemis

Attributes: gambling luck, home protection

Culinary uses: Add aloe vera juice to your favorite smoothie or juice recipe.

Magical uses: Rub 100 percent aloe vera gel on your hands before gambling to bring luck. Dry an aloe vera leaf, grind it well, and add it to home protection spells or mojo bags. Pour aloe vera juice around the perimeter of your property to keep the inhabitants safe.

ANCHOVY

In ancient Rome, the intestines of anchovies were used to create a fermented fish sauce called "garum." Not only was this used to flavor veal and seafood, but it was also applied for hair removal and to treat dog bites and dysentery.

Form: fresh, canned, jarred, paste

Ruler: Venus

Element: Water

Gods: Any Water deities such as Agwé, Ahti, Ikatere, Neptune, Nereus, Pan, Pontus, Poseidon, Ra, Ukupanipo

Goddesses: Any Water deities such as Atargatis, Ishtar, Isis, Venus

Attribute: lust

Culinary uses: Add anchovies to tomato sauces, tomato-based dishes, salad dressings, or any type of fish soup or stew. Anchovy paste has a milder flavor.

Magical uses: Eating anchovies is an aphrodisiac, but the fish-breath might not inspire lust! Add anchovies to a Caesar salad dressing to disguise the flavor a bit.

ANISE

Anise seed tea, called "yansoon," is a common treatment in the Middle East and in Puerto Rico for digestive ailments. In Egypt it's given to nursing mothers to help keep babies free from colic.

Form: dried seed, whole or ground

Ruler: Jupiter

Element: Air

Gods: Apollo, Hermes, Mercury, Ogun, Shango

Goddess: Oya

Attributes: divination, fidelity, luck, nightmare prevention, protection while sleeping, purification

Culinary uses: Flavor cakes, cookies, breads, soups, stews, fruit, lentils, and hot chocolate with anise.

Magical uses: Anise is a perfect ingredient to add to purification baths. Cooking with anise adds love vibrations to your food. Add to sleep pillows or burn seeds before bed to ward off nightmares.

APPLE

Apples are a food with a long and rich history and are mentioned in the mythology of many civilizations. The eleventh Labor of Hercules was to steal the apples from Hera's garden. The Trojan War was started with a golden apple marked "Kallisti" ("For the fairest"). With more than seven thousand different types of apples in the world today, there's no need to fight over them.

Form: whole fresh fruit, dried fruit, juice, cider, dried peel, applesauce

Ruler: Venus

Element: Water

Gods: Apollo, Bes, Dionysus, Frey, Hercules, Lugh, Odin, Olocun, Shango, Teig, Woden, Zeus

Goddesses: Aphrodite, Arwen, Astarte, Athena, Cerridwen, Diana, Eris, Freya, Gaia, Gwen, Hera, Iduna, Ishtar, Ithun, Nemesis, Ochun, Olwyn, Pamona, Venus

Attributes: fidelity, finding a lover, food of the dead, glamour, heartbreak management, hunting, love, lust, romance

Culinary uses: Eat the fresh fruits or make them into applesauce or jelly. Use in pies or muffins or to flavor chicken or pork. Bake them whole or slice in half and grill. Apples are a fine addition to salads.

Magical uses: Bury an apple at each of your doorways or at the graves of loved ones on Samhain (Halloween) to feed the dead. Bake a potential love interest an apple pie with a pinch of pumpkin pie spice to ensure he or she gives you a second look. Create an apple charm by carving a symbol of love into a red apple and allowing it to dry. Use a whole apple as an offering to Venus when petitioning her for a new love or working toward strengthening the bonds of a current one.

APRICOT

In Shakespeare's *A Midsummer Night's Dream*, the fairy Titania takes advantage of the apricot's reputation as an aphrodisiac (along with honey, grapes, and dancing) to lure her beloved.

Form: whole fresh fruit, dried fruit, jelly or jam, pits, apricot kernel oil

Ruler: Venus

Element: Water

Gods: Oko, Shango

Goddesses: Ochun, Venus

Attributes: aphrodisiac, healing, restores energy

Culinary uses: Eat as a fresh fruit or make jam, jellies, or preserves. Slightly warmed jam can be use as a glaze for plain cakes or on chicken. Use in desserts, fruit salads, or chutneys.

Magical uses: Bake chopped dried apricots into "lust muffins" along with freshly diced apple and ginger. Top with a drizzle of melted chocolate and feed to your lover. Dried apricot pits are sometimes used in Vodou magic for healing; add the pit to a mojo bag along with pinch each of peppermint and allspice. Anoint with a dab of olive oil and carry on your person to promote healing.

ARTICHOKE

In Greek mythology, the artichoke was created when Zeus cast his lover Cynara away from Olympus for the crime of secretly visiting her human mother.

Form: fresh, jarred, heart, leaves

Ruler: Mars

Element: Fire

Gods: Jupiter, Zeus

Goddess: Aphrodite

Attributes: aphrodisiac, personal growth, physical protection, spiritual protection

Culinary uses: Artichokes are eaten the world over in many various ways. Steamed, stuffed, boiled, or fried, artichokes are a very versatile food. Vietnam also produces an artichoke tea.

Magical uses: Keep an artichoke on your kitchen windowsill to repel danger of all kinds. When it starts to go bad, throw it out on the compost heap and replace it with another. Add dried artichoke leaves to protection spells or mojo bags. Bury a jar of artichoke hearts near your front door for protection.

ARUGULA

Arugula was recognized as an aphrodisiac as early as the first century AD. Its ability to rev up the libido was written about by Greek philosophers Pliny and Dioscorides.

Form: fresh greens

Ruler: Mars

Element: Fire

God: Priapus

Goddesses: none noted

Attributes: aphrodisiac, success in financial matters

Culinary uses: Add arugula to any green salad for a peppery bite. Add wilted arugula to pasta dishes.

Magical uses: Arugula (sometimes called "rocket") has been used for igniting lust since the days of the Romans; add it to your lust-inducing menu!

ASPARAGUS

Madame de Pompadour, the royal mistress of King Louis XV, furthered not only the popularity of asparagus, but also its reputation for increasing sexual stamina by eating only the tips of the plant, which she called *points d'amour* ("love tips").

Form: fresh

Ruler: Mars

Element: Fire

God: Zeus

Goddess: Perigune

Attributes: prosperity, protection, sexual energy, sexual stamina

Culinary uses: Serve asparagus raw, grilled, steamed, or in stir-fries or mixed into scrambled eggs.

Magical uses: Always eat asparagus from the tips to the stem to gain its magical influence.

AVOCADO

The word *avocado* comes from the Aztec term for "testicle."

Form: whole, pit, oil

Ruler: Venus

Element: Water

God: Orion

Goddesses: Bast, Flora, Hathor

Attributes: anxiety management, aphrodisiac for men, happiness (particularly avocado oil), fertility, love, money draw

Culinary uses: Eat this nutritious and delicious food raw in green salads, as a part of a fruit salad, or sliced and added to sandwiches. Ripe mashed avocado can be made into guacamole or added to smoothies.

Magical uses: Anoint candles, mojo bags, or yourself with avocado oil to promote feelings of happiness. Wrap a dried pit with a dollar bill, tie it with green string, and carry it in your purse to draw money to you. Create a guacamole with mashed avocado, finely diced red onion, coriander, cumin, cilantro, and a pinch of crushed red pepper, and feed it to your lover to spice up the evening!

BAKING SODA

In ancient Egypt, a natural form of sodium bicarbonate, called "natron," was used as a cleaning agent and as an ingredient in mummification. It makes sense that the deities associated with natron would also be associated with its newer form.

Form: powder

Ruler: The Moon

Element: Earth

Gods: Anubis, Horus

Goddess: Nephthys

Attribute: cleansing

Culinary uses: Baking soda is mainly a leavening agent in baking.

Magical uses: Add baking soda to floor sweeps or magical cleaning water. Not only will it help clean magically, but mundanely as well. Add baking soda to cleansing baths. Not only will it get rid of negative energy attached to you, but it softens skin as well! Use baking soda to cast circles where salt might damage plants or concrete.

BANANA

Bananas were introduced to the United States in 1876. So strange was this fruit that instructions on how to use it were included in Todd Goodholme's *Domestic Cyclopedia of Practical Information.* The book instructed readers that bananas could be "eaten raw, either alone or cut in slices with sugar and cream."

Form: fresh fruit, dried fruit, peel

Ruler: Venus

Element: Water

Gods: Ganesha, Kanaloa

Goddesses: Banana Maiden, Brahmani, Durga, Yemaya

Attributes: fertility, prosperity, protection while traveling

Culinary uses: Eat the fruit raw or add it to fruit salads, muffins, or other baked goods. Cover bananas with melted chocolate and freeze for a simple dessert.

Magical uses: Banana peels can wrap up used floor sweeps. Instead of peeling the banana, cut a small opening, scoop out fruit, and then stuff the shell with the used floor sweep. Deposit the whole package into the trash or compost pile.

BARLEY

According to the ancient soothsayer Artemidorus, barley was the first food given to man by the gods.

Form: dried pearls, hot or cold cereals

Ruler: Venus

Element: Earth

Gods: Asar, Bacchus, Dionysus, Indra, Mercury, Osiris, Pellonpekko, Taliesin, Varuna, Vishnu

Goddesses: Albina, Annapurna, Demeter, Isis, Juno, Shala

Attributes: creativity, fertility, love, male sexual stamina, prosperity (especially in business)

Culinary uses: For soups, stews, bread, or beer.

Magical uses: Sprinkle barley around your business or work area to promote financial success, especially if your work is something creativity based. Mix barley with salt to form a circle when doing fertility rituals.

BASIL

Basil plants have been reported throughout time to grow best when they are shouted and cursed at.

Form: fresh leaves, dried ground herb

Ruler: Mars

Element: Fire

Gods: Babalu-Aye, Ellegua, Krishna, Ogun, Shango, Vishnu

Goddesses: Erzulie Fréda Dahomey, Hecate, Hestia, Lakshmi, Ochun, Sekhmet, Tulasi, Yemaya

Attributes: banishing, business success, creativity, exorcism, fertility, fidelity, handfasting or marriage blessings, house blessings, love, love divination, joy, luck, money draw, passion, prosperity, protection, protection during travel, soothes feelings of anger

Culinary uses: Use to create pesto, to flavor pasta dishes, pasta sauces, carrots, chicken, fish, tomatoes, veal, beans, rice, eggs, vegetables, or Italian food.

Magical uses: Keep a basil plant growing on the windowsill of your bedroom to ward off arguments, increase lust, and keep your lover faithful. Inhaling the scent of basil is said to flood the soul with happy feelings; create a basil-infused oil (avocado oil is a good choice) to dab on your skin when you're feeling blue. Throwing a bit of basil under your bed is said to stave off nightmares. Drinking basil tea is said to help a person's ability to communicate with dragons and basilisks. Add a few basil leaves and a sprig of parsley to your bath before sex to ensure that your lover remains faithful to you. Sprinkle dried basil into your wallet or coin jar to attract more money.

BAY LEAF

Here's a household tip: Scatter bay leaves on your windowsills to repel flies or in your pantry to repel roaches.

Form: whole leaves (fresh or dried), ground

Ruler: Sun

Element: Fire

Gods: Adonis, Aesculapius, Apollo, Buddha, Cernunnos, Cupid, Eros, Faunus, Fides, Hermes, Krishna, Ogun, Olocun, Ra, Vishnu, Zeus

Goddesses: Ceres, Cerridwen, Demeter

Attributes: clairvoyance, cleansing, divination, exorcism, healing, luck, lust, money draw, new employment, prophetic dreams, protection, psychic awareness, purification, strength, wisdom and learning, wish magic

Culinary uses: Bay leaves can flavor artichokes, sauces, soups, chicken, pork, fish, potatoes, duck, tomato sauces, stews, and roasts.

Magical uses: Add bay leaves to sleep pillows to promote prophetic dreams. Mix bay leaves and anise and burn over self-lighting charcoal when practicing any form of divination for an instant boost to your psychic abilities.

BEANS

The goddess Demeter is said to look over all vegetable crops with the exception of beans, which were considered by the Greeks to be impure.

Form: dried, raw, cooked

Ruler: Mercury

Element: Air

God: Apollo

Goddesses: Carnea, Demeter, Fabula, Ukemochi, Yansa

Attributes: block psychic abilities, communication, creativity, exorcism, luck, lust, nightmare prevention, offering to the dead, protection against evil, wish magic

Culinary uses: Beans, depending on type, have innumerable applications, from soups, casseroles, alone as a side dish, in chilies, etc.

Magical uses: Old gypsy lore says that carrying a dried bean in your pocket is a powerful lust amulet. Amphiaraus, an ancient clairvoyant, claimed to avoid eating beans because he said that they dimmed his psychic dreams. In ancient Rome, beans were eaten at funerals, as they were thought to hold the souls of the dead. Scattering roasted beans around your home, according to old Japanese lore, will drive out demons.

BEER

Beer is the most easily obtainable form of hops. Beer also contains barley and can be used in its place for some magical purposes.

Form: liquid

Ruler: Mars

Element: Air

Gods: Aegir, Byggvir, Dionysus, Enki, Osiris, Radegast, Raugupatis, Silenus, Tezcatzontecatl

Goddesses: Bast, Goibniu, Hathor, Inanna, Mbaba Mwana Waresa, Ninkasi, Raugutiene, Sekhmet, Tenenit, Tjenenet, Yasigi

Attributes: cleansing, health/healing, hex breaking (especially in bath form), peaceful sleep, relaxation

Culinary uses: Marinate beef with beer or flavor chili. Beer is often an ingredient in baking bread.

Magical uses: Place a small glass of beer on your altar when doing healing rituals. Anoint sleep pillows with beer. A beer poured into the tub while you are filling it creates a powerful cleansing bath.

BEET

Sharing a beet is said to make two people fall helplessly in love.

Form: fresh, juice

Ruler: Saturn

Element: Earth

Gods: none noted

Goddess: Astarte

Attributes: banishing negativity, love

Culinary uses: Beets can be pickled or shredded for use in various salads.

Magical uses: Add sliced beets to a green salad to promote loving feelings. Substitute beet juice in any magical formula for love that calls for blood. It is a tradition in the Jewish faith to eat beets on Rosh Hashanah while saying a prayer for their enemies to be removed. Try adding beets to your table when you need to remove something negative from your life.

BERGAMOT

While not easily found alone in the spice aisle, it's simple enough to pick up in the tea aisle as an ingredient in Earl Grey.

Form: dried flower

Ruler: Mercury

Element: Air

Gods: Ellegua, Shango

Goddesses: Persephone, Rhiannon

Attributes: helps boost confidence, helps overcome addictions and breaks bad habits, kickstarts energy level, protects during travel, retention of information when studying

Culinary uses: Bergamot is a flavoring for fish, chicken, soups, or yogurt.

Magical uses: Substitute bergamot in any magical formula that calls for lemon balm.

BLACKBERRY

Old English folklore claims that blackberries should never be picked after October 11 (Old Michaelmas Day), because on that day, the devil urinates on them. In reality, the cooler weather of October often encouraged mold to set in on the fruit.

Form: fresh, frozen, jelly, syrup

Ruler: Venus

Element: Water

God: Lugh

Goddesses: Brighid, Venus

Attributes: creativity, lust, prosperity, protection

Culinary uses: Blackberries are good in cobblers and pies or as jams or jellies. Cook blackberries down to add to sauces, both sweet and savory. Top hot or cold cereals, yogurt, ice cream, or pound cake with fresh (or thawed frozen) fruit.

Magical uses: Eat blackberries before or during creative endeavors, as both Lugh and Brighid are patrons of art and crafts. Serve a pie made with a mix of blackberries and apples to inspire lusty impulses in your partner. Blackberries are appropriate to serve for either Lughnasadh or Imbolc, as they are sacred to deities of those sabbats. Pour blackberry syrup over buckwheat pancakes to promote prosperity in your household.

BLACK PEPPER

At one point in time, black pepper was traded ounce for ounce with gold.

Form: whole or ground

Ruler: Mars

Element: Fire

Gods: Ares, Horus, Mars, Montu, Oko, Shango

Goddess: Hecate

Attributes: banishment, exorcism, hex breaking, protection

Culinary uses: Black pepper brings out the flavor in just about all savory dishes. When cooking with black pepper, sprinkle it on toward the end of the process to retain its flavor.

Magical uses: Combine equal parts ground black pepper, dried basil, and dried garlic powder with a pinch of cayenne; sprinkle this mixture around the outside of your home for protection and to ward off any ill will being sent your way.

BLUEBERRY

Tossing a handful of blueberries in the path of a foe is said to cause them discord.

Form: fresh, dried, syrup, frozen, jam, or jelly

Ruler: Venus

Element: Water

Gods: Dagda, Lugh

Goddess: Brighid

Attributes: protection from psychic attack

Culinary uses: Add to breads, muffins, or bagels. Use to create cobblers, pies, jams, or jellies. Top hot or cold cereals, yogurt, ice cream, or pound cake with fresh (or thawed frozen) fruit.

Magical uses: Crush blueberries and paint protective symbols onto bare skin with the juice. Allow the juice to set and stain, then wash off (always try a small dab first to check for an allergic reaction before going hog wild with this). Anoint sleep pillows with a bit of blueberry juice to lend its power; alternately add dried blueberries directly to the pillow.

BRAZIL NUT

Brazil nuts are known for attracting people to you. Next time you're participating in a social activity, carry a whole one in your pocket and let it do its thing.

Form: whole nut

Ruler: Mercury

Element: Air

Gods: none noted

Goddesses: none noted

Attributes: friendship, prosperity

Culinary uses: Eat whole raw or roasted nuts. Brazil nuts can replace walnuts in most any recipe.

Magical uses: String a cord through a Brazil nut and wear this around your neck when seeking to attract paying, friendly customers. Chop Brazil nuts and add to a fruit salad featuring clementines or oranges; share this with a friend to strengthen the bond between the two of you.

BREAD

People have been offering bread to the divine for thousands of years. The Egyptians even offered it to their sacred cats. So many superstitions and folk magics are attached to bread that they could fill a book of their own! One of my favorites: the Swedish custom that you won't marry until you are able to cut straight slices of bread.

Form: loaves, slices, croutons, bread crumbs, pizza crust, corn bread, pita, crackers

Ruler: Moon

Element: Earth

God: Osiris

Goddesses: Ceres, Demeter, Dugnai, Fornax, Hestia, Isis

Attributes: fertility, giving thanks, prosperity, protection

Culinary uses: Breads can be created with a variety of ingredients and flavoring. Practice baking with different types of flour, fruits, nuts, herbs, and spices to find baked goods perfect for your needs. Serve your baked bread as French toast, bread pudding, croutons, or sandwiches.

Magical uses: Bread makes the perfect vehicle for culinary magic. It can be twisted into a variety of shapes before baking, and the items you can add to it for both flavor and magical intent are endless. Make lusty apple muffins with cloves and cinnamon to serve to your lover. Banana bread with wheat flour, honey, and eggs makes a powerful fertility loaf. Mix up a batch of your favorite corn muffin recipe. To the batter, make sure to add diced onion, black pepper, salt, and a pinch of sage. When the muffins are done cooking, take the best-looking four and place one at each of the four corners of your land to enhance the protection of your property. Make a sandwich on caraway seed–topped rye bread and share it with someone you need to have better communication with. Share stale bread scraps (or cook an extra loaf just for this use) with the birds outside your home. I have a daily tradition of tossing bread out my kitchen window and saying, "In thanks, I feed your family as you feed mine." It reminds me to be grateful for what my family has and is an act of gratitude to the God and Goddess. When moving into a new house, bread should be one of the first items carried in to ensure the home will always be filled with food.

BROCCOLI

Ancient Romans nicknamed broccoli "the five green fingers of Jupiter."

Form: fresh, frozen

Ruler: Moon

Element: Water

God: Jupiter

Goddesses: Artemis, Diana, Flora, Luna

Attributes: spiritual protection

Culinary uses: Broccoli is an endlessly versatile food. Eat it raw with dip or chopped into almost any type of salad. Steamed or lightly boiled it can be served simply with butter, salt, and pepper or with a luscious cheese sauce. Use in stir-fries, omelets, or quiches.

Magical uses: Grow broccoli in your garden for protection (it's easier to grow than you'd think!). Add broccoli and brussels sprouts to a meal when you feel the need to boost your spiritual protection.

BRUSSELS SPROUTS

According to Roman mythology, cabbages originated from the tears of Lycurgus, king of the Edoni in Thrace.

Form: fresh

Ruler: Moon

Element: Water

Gods: none noted

Goddess: Flora

Attribute: spiritual protection

Culinary uses: Brussels sprouts can be boiled, steamed, sautéed, or roasted. Remove a few of the outside leaves to keep them from being tough. Cut an "X" in the bottom with a knife to ensure that they cook evenly.

Magical uses: String a batch of brussels sprouts with a needle and fishing line; place in a dehydrator (or hang) and allow to dry. Hang somewhere inconspicuous in your home as a protection charm. When you feel you are entering into any situation where you might need spiritual protection, remove a brussels sprout from the string and carry it in your pocket.

BUCKWHEAT

Though many people believe buckwheat to be a cereal grain, it isn't. It's a fruit seed, making it suitable for those who are sensitive to grains or gluten.

Form: flour, noodles (soba), kasha (toasted buckwheat)

Ruler: Venus

Element: Earth

Gods: Jupiter, Krishna

Goddess: Epona

Attributes: new employment, prosperity

Culinary uses: Buckwheat makes pancakes or gluten-free beer. Incorporate buckwheat noodles into Japanese or Korean dishes, or substitute for other noodles in Italian meals.

Magical uses: Buckwheat can replace salt to cast circles of magical protection. To help ensure a fair shot at a new job, dust buckwheat onto your hands before your interview. Make sure to not wash it completely off before shaking hands with your potential employer. Though buckwheat has a correspondence with prosperity, it isn't a food that will bring you riches, but instead it ensures that your cupboards will never go bare. Keep a container of buckwheat mixed with alfalfa in your pantry to help ensure that you will always have enough to feed your family.

BUTTER

In medieval Ireland, kegs of butter were buried in peat bogs for preservation. Now called "bog butter," it was so immune to rot that there are still samples to be found in museums.

Form: stick, tub, melted

Ruler: Venus

Element: Water

Gods: Agni, Brahma, Krishna, Prajapati, Vishnu

Goddesses: Hathor, Lakshmi, Venus

Attributes: prosperity, protection

Culinary uses: Spread butter on breads or muffins. Butter can add flavor to cooked vegetables. Sauté foods that cook quickly in butter.

Magical uses: Take advantage of butter's prosperity and protection energies by creating and eating "beurre composé" or compound butters. Bring butter to room temperature, then whip it together with your choice of herbs. Use immediately or refrigerate. Use compound butters on cooked meat, to top vegetables, on baked potatoes, or on fish.

CABBAGE

In the British Isles there was once a custom for girls to pull up a cabbage on Halloween. The roots of the cabbage would divine what sort of man the girl would eventually marry.

Form: fresh

Ruler: Moon

Element: Water

God: Egres

Goddess: Flora

Attributes: house blessing, prosperity, protection

Culinary uses: Chop roughly or shred into salads or coleslaw. Add to soups, make cabbage rolls, or pickle cabbage to make sauerkraut or spicy kimchi.

Magical uses: When moving into a new home, the first plant you should bring into the house is a cabbage. It's said that this will bless your new home and any gardens that might grow there. Don't eat your house blessing cabbage, but instead compost it, so that its blessing will keep adding to your yard and plants.

CARAWAY SEED

Though caraway seed is now commonly used to flavor rye bread, it was once thought to be very unlucky to use caraway seed in your bread.

Form: dried seeds

Ruler: Mercury

Element: Air

God: Shango

Goddesses: none noted

Attributes: communication, fidelity, lust, mental clarity, study aid, theft prevention, protection, wisdom

Culinary uses: Caraway seeds flavor apples, bacon, beef, curries, rye bread, duck, cheese, potatoes, sausages, sauerkraut.

Magical uses: Keep a bit of caraway seed in your glove box to protect your car and its contents. Sprinkle a powdered mix of caraway and basil on your lover's shoes to make sure he or she returns to you. Grind a mix of caraway and rosemary to burn when studying to help retain information. Strew a mix of caraway seeds, rosemary, anise, and marjoram in the path of those getting handfasted or married to bless them with love, fidelity, and good communication.

CARDAMOM

Cardamom is used around the world as an additive to coffee and is one of the primary ingredients in chai.

Form: pods, dried seeds

Ruler: Venus

Element: Air

God: Vishnu

Goddesses: Erzulie Fréda, Hecate, Lakshmi

Attributes: love and lust (especially when added to wine), prosperity (especially when burned)

Culinary uses: Cardamom adds flavor to apples, chicken, coffee, curries, lamb, mulled wines, rice, stews, various seafood.

Magical uses: Create a tradition of indulging in a red wine mulled with cardamom and crushed coriander alongside some good quality chocolate on your anniversary. It will help cement your bonds and rekindle your passions!

CAYENNE

Hot peppers, including cayenne, were thought to be one of the best weapons against vampires and werewolves. Dried peppers were burned to keep the creatures of the night at bay. Even today you can find strings of dried peppers hanging in kitchens for protection.

Form: ground, dried herb; whole pepper

Ruler: Mars

Element: Fire

God: Ellegua

Goddesses: none specifically noted, but can be used when honoring any goddess associated with Fire

Attributes: hex-breaking, lust, protection

Culinary uses: Cayenne can be added to Mexican foods, potatoes, eggs, barbecue sauce.

Magical uses: Hang dried peppers on a string for protection. Add a pinch of ground cayenne to a meal for your lover to spice things up.

CHAMOMILE

Look for packaged whole chamomile flowers in the Latin spices area of your supermarket. Alternately, look for chamomile tea.

Form: dried, tea bags

Ruler: Sun

Element: Water

Gods: Cernunnos, Lugh, Ra, Woden

Goddess: Ochun

Attributes: aids in meditation, anger management, cleansing, enhances psychic dreams, money draw, promotes feelings of happiness, prosperity, relaxation, restful sleep

Culinary uses: Chamomile flowers make a delicious and relaxing tea before bed.

Magical uses: Add several tea bags directly to a warm bath to relax and cleanse yourself before doing any magical works. Combine chamomile and other money drawing and luck herbs; grind well. Rub a bit between your hands before gambling.

CHEESE

In Greek myth, Aristaeus gave the gift of cheese to humans. In Homer's *Odyssey*, the cyclops Polyphemus made cheese.

Form: blocks, wedges, slices, hard, soft, grated

Ruler: Moon

Element: Water

God: Aristaeus

Goddess: Saulé

Attribute: love

Culinary uses: From the simplest cheese and crackers to the most elaborate lasagna, cheeses are used in innumerable recipes and pairings.

Magical uses: Create a Caesar salad with lust-inducing anchovies, parmesan cheese, and mustard in the dressing. It's sure to turn things spicy!

CHIVES

In medieval times, bundles of chives were hung from doorways to ward off evil.

Form: fresh, dried, frozen

Ruler: Mars

Element: Fire

Gods: none noted

Goddesses: none noted

Attributes: creative blockage buster, heartbreak ease, motivational, protection

Culinary uses: Add raw to potato dishes, green salads, egg dishes, soups, or dips.

Magical uses: Grow a small pot of chives in any room in which you need to feel motivated and creative.

CHOCOLATE (CACAO)

According to Aztec myth, Quetzalcoatl delivered cacao beans to humans from heaven. For some time, cacao beans were used as currency; four beans would purchase a pumpkin.

Form: bars, powdered, syrup

Ruler: Venus

Element: Water

Gods: Ek Chuah, Hobnil, Quetzalcoatl

Goddesses: Chantico, Xochiquetzal

Attributes: love, lust, offering to the dead

Culinary uses: Though mainly used to make sweets and baked goods, chocolate is also used in some savory dishes, such as chicken mole.

Magical uses: Add chocolate to your ancestor altar, especially during Dia de los Muertos (Day of the Dead). Chocolate creates feelings of lust and love in women.

CILANTRO

Though the plant itself is called cilantro, the seeds of the cilantro plant are better known as the spice coriander.

Form: fresh

Ruler: Mercury

Element: Fire

God: Obatala

Goddess: Ochun

Attributes: communication, creativity, mental awareness, new employment opportunities, prosperity of creative projects

Culinary uses: Cilantro flavors many Mexican or Asian recipes. Cilantro is an essential ingredient in fresh salsas. Substitute cilantro for basil in a pesto recipe. Add cilantro to softened butter and brush onto corn on the cob.

Magical uses: Sprinkle dried cilantro around the area where you apply your creativity. Alternately, keep fresh cilantro, stems down, in a glass of water on your desk or work space. Build a menu featuring foods that include cilantro when hosting a social situation to create a positive atmosphere.

CINNAMON

Greek legend states the belief that cinnamon was collected from the nests of the phoenix.

Form: stick, ground

Ruler: Mercury

Element: Fire

Gods: Helios, Ra, Surya

Goddesses: Aphrodite, Bast, Ochun, Oya, Venus

Attributes: creativity, fidelity, health/healing, love, lust, money draw, protection, psychic abilities, purification, successful work

Culinary uses: Cinnamon is a flavoring for apples, brandy, chicken, chocolates, puddings, pork, peaches, winter squash, yams, sweet potatoes, various baked goods, cinnamon toast, French toast.

Magical uses: Create an infused oil with cinnamon and anoint your creative or work tools with it to ensure creative energy and business success. Cinnamon can be substituted in any magical formula calling for cassia.

CLOVES

Much of the aromatic essential oil of cloves is lost when they are ground. Choose whole cloves when you can and grind them yourself in a spice or coffee grinder or with a mortar and pestle.

Form: whole or ground

Ruler: Jupiter

Element: Fire

Gods: Ellegua, Obatala, Oko

Goddesses: Lavangi, Oya

Attributes: attraction, heartbreak ease, helps end gossip, helps you to obtain your desire, love, memory enhancer, prosperity

Culinary uses: Cloves can be added to apples, baked beans, ham, mulled cider or wine, sweet potatoes, yams, pies.

Magical uses: Cloves are potent in spells when your need to get your way or sway someone to your side in a situation. Cover a tablespoon of whole cloves with sunflower oil; drain. Anoint a candle with this oil when working to stop a gossip in his or her tracks.

COCONUT

The liquid contained in a coconut is completely sterile until it's cracked open. In an emergency, it can even be used for intravenous hydration.

Form: flour, milk, shredded, water, whole

Ruler: Venus

Element: Water

Gods: Osiris, Sri, Te Tuna, Varuna

Goddesses: any lunar goddess, Isis, Neititua Abinem

Attributes: fertility, purification

Culinary uses: Coconut products have a variety of culinary applications. Coconut meat is often used in candies, confections, and baked goods. Coconut water is becoming popular as a sports drink. Coconut milk is found in frozen drinks and is added to curries.

Magical uses: Coconuts are often thrown into the sea as an offering to various water deities. In some magical practices, a coconut is rolled across the floor with a broom to purify a room of negativity. Add a handful of unsweetened coconut flakes or a bottle of coconut water to purification baths or floor washes. Use coconut milk in recipes when trying to get pregnant.

COFFEE

In Ethiopia, Kenya, and Somalia, the Oromo people once planted coffee trees on the graves of sorcerers. The plant that grew was thought to be due in part to the tears their god wept over the body.

Form: instant, grounds, brewed

Ruler: Mars

Element: Fire

God: Ellegua

Goddess: Ishtar

Attributes: creativity, energy enhancer, love, road opener

Culinary uses: Add a tablespoon of leftover brewed coffee to any chocolate-based recipe to enhance the flavor of the chocolate.

Magical uses: Add leftover brewed coffee to your bath to get energized. To create a simmering incense to get your creative juices flowing, combine ground coffee, cinnamon, and orange peel in a pan. Cover with water and simmer over low heat (never leave unattended).

CORIANDER

Coriander is one of the oldest known herbs and has been found in Egyptian tombs as funerary offerings.

Form: dried herb

Ruler: Mars

Element: Fire

God: Obatala

Goddesses: Hathor, Ochun

Attributes: love, lust, mental awareness

Culinary uses: Coriander adds flavor to chicken, fish, mushrooms, polenta, sausage, curries.

Magical uses: Coriander is a powerful aphrodisiac, especially when brewed into a warm drink. Try it in coffee or tea or use it in a mulled red wine to share with your lover.

CORN

Without the intervention of humans in the form of cultivation, corn as we know it today would not exist. It is not a plant that grows naturally in the wild, and it can't reproduce without the help of farmers.

Form: fresh on the cob, canned, frozen, cornmeal, corn flour, cornstarch, corn-based cereals, corn oil, dried corn husks, popcorn

Ruler: Venus

Element: Earth

Gods: Adonis, Centeotl, Centzon Totochtin, Dionysus, Fast-ta-chee, Gwion, Oko, Osiris, Quetzalcoatl, Tlazopilli, Xochipilli, Yum Caax

Goddesses: Ashan, Ceres, Chicomecoatl, Corn Mother, Hecate, Isis, Iyatiku, Kornjunfer, Nepit, Onatha, Perigune, Selu, Xilonen, Yellow Woman

Attributes: ancestor offering (especially when petitioning for financial help), fertility, love, prosperity, protection

Culinary uses: Corn products have a wide variety of applications. Fresh corn can be eaten after a quick boil or cooked and added to salads or salsas. Corn flour can thicken chili and give it a rich flavor, or it can be made into tortillas.

Magical uses: Cornmeal, corn flour, or cornstarch can be the base to almost any floor sweep, but especially those meant for prosperity. Leave a dried stalk of corn on your ancestor altar in the fall.

CRUSHED RED PEPPER

Though crushed red pepper and cayenne powder come from the same species of hot pepper, because of the way they are produced, they are not completely interchangeable for cooking purposes. They can, however, be used in the same way for magical purposes.

Form: dried

Ruler: Mars

Element: Fire

God: Ellegua

Goddesses: none specifically noted, but can be used to honor any goddess of Fire

Attributes: hex breaking, lust, protection

Culinary uses: Crushed red pepper can spice up a variety of foods: soups, marinades, omelets, pasta dishes, and homemade sausages to name a few. It's also perfect for sprinkling on top of pizzas!

Magical uses: Sprinkle a bit of crushed red pepper around your property line to boost your home's protection. Add crushed red pepper to meals you feed to your lover to spice up the evening.

CUMIN

Cumin is not only said to keep your lover faithful, but folklore also claims that when it is fed to chickens, it will keep them from wandering as well.

Form: ground

Ruler: Mars or Venus

Element: Fire

Gods: Ellegua, Olocun, Shango

Goddesses: Lakshmi, Ochun, Yemaya

Attributes: banishment, fidelity, love, lust, promotes feelings of security, protection, theft prevention

Culinary uses: Cumin flavors barbecue sauce, beans, Mexican foods, beef, chicken, corn, curries, avocados, chili.

Magical uses: Add a bit of cumin to any protection bags you create for your home or automobile. Add a pinch of cumin to your favorite barbecue sauce to promote lusty feelings in your partner—and to help ensure that they won't stray!

DILL

Burning dill is said to make clouds clear from the skies and end thunderstorms.

Form: fresh, dried

Ruler: Mercury

Element: Fire

God: Adammair

Goddesses: none noted

Attributes: fertility, friendship, hex breaking, love, protection against ghosts, truthfulness, weather magic

Culinary uses: Dips, coleslaw, pickles, eggs, pasta or potato salads, salad dressings, and tuna salad can be flavored with dill. Add fresh dill to green salads.

Magical uses: Add to charm bags hung near your front door to keep out unwanted spirits. Sprinkle in a circle around your bed for protection while you sleep. Serve in food when you want someone to be truthful with you. It's said that carrying dill near your heart will protect against hexes.

EGGS

Beware: it's said to be bad luck to bring eggs into a house after dark!

Form: raw, cooked, shells

Ruler: Moon

Element: Water

Gods: Brahma, Hansa, Hiranyagarbha, Pemba

Goddesses: Astara, Eostre, Hathor, Knosuano, Luonnotar, Saulé

Attributes: absorbs negativity, fertility, hex breaking, rebirth, wish magic

Culinary uses: Eggs can be added to various baked goods, or fried, scrambled, boiled, or poached. Turn boiled eggs into deviled eggs or egg salad. Sliced or chopped, eggs can be added to green salads, pasta salad, or potato salad.

Magical uses: Create chalk from washed, dried, and crushed eggshells to draw veves, runes, or sigils during rituals. Add eggshell powdser to cornstarch and dust this on the body to magically promote fertility. Gently roll an egg through the house to absorb negativity.

FENNEL SEED

When Prometheus stole fire from the gods, he brought it to humans carried in a fennel seed stalk.

Form: dried

Ruler: Mercury

Element: Fire

Gods: Adonis, Dionysus, Pan, Prometheus

Goddesses: none noted

Attributes: abundance, love, physical healing, protection (especially during travel), spiritual healing, study aid

Culinary uses: Fennel seed can flavor sauces, Mediterranean or Middle Eastern cuisine, pasta, or vegetables.

Magical uses: Hang a pouch of fennel seed near your door at Midsummer to keep fairies from entering your home. Grind fennel seed and rosemary and burn over self-lighting charcoal while studying to help retain information.

FLAXSEED/OIL

Flaxseeds will last longer when stored in the refrigerator or freezer.

Form: whole or ground seed, oil

Ruler: Jupiter

Element: Fire

Gods: Egres, Vaizgantas

Goddesses: Hulda, Saulé

Attributes: fertility, healing, new employment, peaceful home, prosperity in business, protection (especially during pregnancy and of children)

Culinary uses: Add flax to hot or cold cereals. Sprinkle on bread right before baking. Because of its high oil content, flaxseed can be substituted for the oil in some baked goods at a 3:1 ratio (seed to oil).

Magical uses: Burn flax over self-lighting charcoal when sewing, spinning, or weaving to ask for Hulda's blessing, as she is the goddess who taught humans how to spin and weave cloth. Stuff a mojo bag or poppet with flax, and carry it with you during a job interview or set it near where you do business.

GARLIC

In ancient times garlic was often added to wedding bouquets to help keep evil spirits at bay.

Form: fresh, dried, and chopped or ground

Ruler: Mars

Element: Fire

Gods: Ellegua, Mars

Goddesses: Bear Goddess, Hecate

Attributes: exorcism, fertility, healing, love, protection, repels evil and illness

Culinary uses: Add garlic to almost any savory dish: pasta, rice, tomatoes, beef, chicken, seafood, vegetables.

Magical uses: Separate the cloves of a garlic head and add to a jar. Fill with apple cider vinegar and let set for several weeks to create a simple Four Thieves Vinegar. Sprinkle over your doorstep to keep out illness and negativity. Stored in the kitchen, garlic is said to keep accidents while cooking at bay. Garlic can substitute in any magical formula that calls for wolfsbane. Skip the garlic before working with the goddess Cybele, the god Nabu, or any Hindu deities, as those who ate garlic were not allowed into their temples or shrines.

GINGER

If you're creating a magical spell or work that you'd like to manifest quickly, add a bit of ginger to the mix to hasten your magic along.

Form: fresh or dried and ground

Ruler: Mars

Element: Fire

God: Shango

Goddess: The Morrigan

Attributes: adds strength to any magical work, commitment, courage, energy, healing, luck, lust, money draw, personal power, physical strength, success

Culinary uses: Ginger adds flavor to Asian recipes, gingerbread, cookies, pumpkin pie. Fresh ginger makes a wonderful tea.

Magical uses: Ginger can substitute for mandrake or galangal in any magical recipe. Pop a piece of candied ginger in your mouth before any ritual or magical work to increase your personal energy and power. Keep a small dish near your cash register filled with ginger, allspice, and cinnamon to draw money to your business.

HONEY

Priestesses of Artemis and Demeter were often referred to as "bees."

Form: liquid

Ruler: Venus

Element: Water

Gods: Ah-Muzen-Cab, Aristaeus (The Honey Lord), Babilos, Ea, Kama, Min, Nishiki Pas, Pan, Ra, Zosim

Goddesses: Aphrodite, Artemis, Austeia, Cybele, Demeter, Mellonia, Meritta, Nantosvelta, Nishkende Tevtyar, Ochun, Potnia

Attributes: ancestor offering (especially when petitioning for help with financial matters), fertility, healing, love, luck

Culinary uses: Honey can be spread on breads or other baked goods. It is a substitute for sugar. Add to homemade barbecue sauces or honey mustard.

Magical uses: A bit of honey acts as a binder for homemade incense. If offering honey to a deity or your ancestors, it's important to taste the honey before leaving it as proof that it's not poisoned.

LEMON

An old wives' tale states that if a pregnant woman craves lemons or lemonade, she will give birth to a son.

Form: fresh fruit, peel, juice, rind, oil

Ruler: Moon

Element: Water

God: Jambhala

Goddesses: Amaterasu, Yemaya

Attributes: cleansing, exorcism (especially of poltergeists), friendship, love, lunar magic, protection during sleep, purification

Culinary uses: Juice lemons to create lemonade or to sprinkle on fruits or veggies to keep them from turning brown after being cut. The juice or rind can be used to flavor fish, rice, candies, cookies, chicken, pasta.

Magical uses: Add a splash of lemon juice to floor and/or wall washes. Serve lemonade at social gatherings to help develop feelings of friendship. Dry slices of lemon in a low oven or in a food dehydrator. Add the slices to a wreath to hang over your bed for protection while you sleep. Lemon peel substitutes for lemon balm, lemongrass, or citron in magical formulas.

LEMONGRASS

Lemongrass essential oil is an important part of the hoodoo traditional recipe for Chinese Wash, used to cleanse the home of negativity. Make your own household version by brewing a cup of strong lemongrass tea with a thick slice of ginger. Let it steep for about ten minutes, then pour into a bucket of warm water along with a good splash of your favorite pine-based cleaner.

Form: fresh, dried

Ruler: Moon

Element: Water

God: Mercury

Goddesses: Diana, Ochun

Attributes: healing, love, mental clarity, purification, strengthens psychic abilities

Culinary uses: Lemongrass flavors Southeast Asian recipes, including curries, sauces, and soups. As lemongrass doesn't soften when cooked, remove it before serving.

Magical uses: Pour hot water over lemongrass and let it steep for fifteen minutes; then strain. Cleanse your ritual tools used in divination with the liquid. Lemongrass can be substituted in most magical formulas calling for mugwort.

MARJORAM

Venus is said to have brought marjoram to earth.

Form: fresh or dried

Ruler: Venus

Element: Earth

God: Horus

Goddesses: Aphrodite, Venus

Attributes: heartbreak ease, love, luck, lust, protection

Culinary uses: Marjoram flavors sausages, herbal breads, green salads, and eggs.

Magical uses: Place marjoram on your altar to honor Venus, or add it to any love magics to garner her blessings. Carry marjoram with you when in mourning as it helps a person to return to happiness.

MILK

The correspondences for this listing refer to basic cow's milk. Find more information on different types of milk listed under "Soy" and "Coconut."

Form: liquid, dried, flavored, sweetened condensed, evaporated

Ruler: Venus

Element: Water

Gods: Ellegua, Krishna

Goddesses: Anu, Bat, Britannia, Damona, Ethne, Galatea, Hathor, Hera, Hesat Kamadhenu, Mehet-Weret, Nut, Prithvi

Attributes: prosperity, protection, purification

Culinary uses: Drink milk alone or add it into sauces, soups, puddings, smoothies, or in the breading process of fried foods.

Magical uses: Milk has been traditionally used to ritually bathe images of deities; dab a bit of milk on statues to purify them.

MOLASSES

In 1919 a tank filled with molasses burst in Boston, Massachusetts. The tank held over two million gallons of molasses and caused a wave of more than eight feet in height, moving at thirty-five miles per hour.

Form: liquid

Ruler: Mars

Element: Earth

God: Shango

Goddesses: Oya, Yemaya

Attributes: ancestor offering (especially when petitioning for help with financial matters), money draw, prosperity for business

Culinary uses: Molasses can be used to flavor baked beans, gingerbread, and in the creation of dark, heavy ales.

Magical uses: Leave a bottle of molasses on your workstation or near your cash register or tip jar to draw money to you. Molasses is one of the goddess Yemaya's favorite offerings.

MUSTARD SEED

If you find yourself with a bottle you'd like to reuse, but it has an unpleasant odor, place a spoonful of prepared mustard into the bottle, then fill it with hot water. Give it a good shake, empty, and wash with your favorite dish soap. The smell will be gone for good!

Form: dried seeds, ground powder, condiment

Ruler: Mars

Element: Fire

Gods: Aesculapius, Buddha

Goddess: Lakshmi

Attributes: fertility, lust, mental clarity, protection from ghosts, remembrance

Culinary uses: Mustard seeds add flavor to a salad dressing, deviled eggs, and sauces. Use as a condiment on sandwiches.

Magical uses: Add a pinch of mustard seed to rosemary to create a study incense to help you retain information. Sprinkle powdered mustard in the path of someone you'd like to inspire lust in. Sprinkle a mix of mustard seeds and dill across your doorway to keep ghosts from entering your home, especially in the fall months.

NUTMEG

One of the nicknames for the state of Connecticut is "The Nutmeg State," though no one knows quite why the connection was made.

Form: whole, ground

Ruler: Jupiter

Element: Fire

Gods: none noted

Goddesses: Durga, Oya

Attributes: attraction magic, health/healing, helps with divination, luck, lust, money draw, prosperity, strengthens psychic ability

Culinary uses: Nutmeg can flavor Indian or Middle Eastern cuisine or custards, puddings, baked goods, or sauces that include cheese. It's often sprinkled on eggnog and, in Caribbean countries, rum.

Magical uses: Add a whole nutmeg to the bag in which you store your tarot cards or runes to enhance your abilities when using them. Drill a hole through a whole nutmeg and run a string through it to wear as a healing charm. Mix a half teaspoon of powdered nutmeg with a tablespoon of cornstarch to create a gamblers' hand powder. Simply rub a bit of powder over your hands for added luck!

NUTS

See almond, peanut, and walnut.

OATS

In some Eastern European countries, the person who cuts the last sheaf of oats is called "the goat." He has to carry the name until the next year's harvest when another goat will be crowned.

Form: oatmeal, oat flour, various cereals

Ruler: Venus

Element: Earth

Gods: Wirancannos, any harvest Gods

Goddesses: Brighid, Ceres, Demeter

Attributes: ancestor offering (especially when petitioning for help in financial matters), new employment, prosperity

Culinary uses: Oats are helpful in bread making, cookies and granola, or brewing beer.

Magical uses: Bake oat bread at Mabon or the fall equinox, leaving a piece on your altar overnight as an offering for the Goddess. In the morning, throw the bread outside to feed the local birds. Got a job interview? Have a hearty bowl of oatmeal before heading out.

OLIVE/OLIVE OIL

The ancient Egyptians believed that Isis brought the knowledge of how to grow and use olives to humans. The Greeks, however, consider the gift to have come from Athena.

Form: fruit, liquid

Ruler: Sun

Element: Fire

Gods: Apollo, Aristaeus, Brahma, Cupid, Eros, Hermes, Indra, Mars, Mercury, Pan, Poseidon, Ra, Wotan

Goddesses: Aphrodite, Athena, Isis, Minerva, Nut, Ochun, Pax

Attributes: health/healing, house blessings, luck, lust, prosperity, protection

Culinary uses: The kitchen applications of olive oil are innumerable. Add to salad dressings; use to sauté; mix with herbs for a dip with hearty breads. Use for marinades or drizzled over pasta.

Magical uses: Olive oil can be the base for almost any magically infused oil. Olive oil can be your anointing oil when working with Greek deities. It substitutes for mineral oil in any magical formulas.

ONION

Onions appear in ancient Egyptian art more than any other plant.

Form: fresh in any variety, scallions, shallots, dried and ground

Ruler: Mars

Element: Fire

Gods: Horus, Osiris

Goddess: Befana

Attributes: banishment, cleansing, protection

Culinary uses: Onions are an indispensable vegetable for cooking and come in a variety of flavors. Raw onions can be a sandwich topping or part of a salad. Cooked, onions add flavor to sauces, soups, stews, stir-fries, meat, or vegetable dishes. Onions are found in cuisines around the world.

Magical uses: Leave a whole onion on a windowsill to collect negative energy from your home. When it starts to rot, throw it away or add it to your compost pile. For a quick home cleansing, add sliced onions to dishes filled with vinegar and leave them throughout the house for a few hours. Sprinkle dried and diced onion from your spice rack around the outside of your home for instant protective energies.

ORANGE

Orange blossoms carried in a bridal bouquet are said to bring luck in love to the bride and groom.

Form: whole fruit, peel, rind, juice

Ruler: Sun

Element: Fire

Gods: Apollo, Cernunnos

Goddesses: Hera, Naavri, Pamona

Attributes: ancestor offering, cleansing, confidence, creativity, friendship, glamour, health/healing, love, prosperity, success

Culinary uses: Eat oranges by hand. Orange slices can be added to fresh salads or desserts. Orange zest, fruit, or juice can be used to flavor baked goods, sauces, marinades, jams, and jellies.

Magical uses: Add dried orange peel to a bath when you want to attract love or friendship. Grind dried orange peel, lemon peel, and a vanilla bean together; burn this incense during social gatherings to strengthen bonds of friendship. Dried orange peel can be substituted in any magical formula that calls for citron, saffron, or neroli.

OREGANO

According to Greek mythology, Aphrodite created the oregano plant as a symbol of happiness. The word *oregano* translates to "joy of the mountain."

Form: fresh, dried

Ruler: Jupiter

Element: Air

Gods: none noted

Goddesses: Aphrodite, Artemis

Attributes: health/healing, joy, love, luck, money draw

Culinary uses: Oregano flavors Italian recipes, Mexican recipes, tomato dishes, beef, poultry, chili, soups, or stews.

Magical uses: Create a wreath from fresh branches of oregano for your front door to bring feelings of joy to all who enter your home.

PARSLEY

Though it has a much better reputation in modern times, in ancient times parsley had a bad name. Ancient Greeks associated this herb with death, as it was thought to have grown from the blood of Archemorus, also known as "the forerunner of death." In England the gallows rope was sometimes referred to as "Welsh parsley."

Form: flat leaf, curly, fresh, dried

Ruler: Mercury

Element: Air

Gods: Archemorus, Zeus

Goddess: Persephone

Attributes: exorcism of negative energy, love, fertility, fidelity, lust, protection, purification

Culinary uses: Add parsley to sauces, broths, or herbal butters. Chopped raw parsley can be a finishing touch to almost any savory dish.

Magical uses: Add parsley to a purification bath, along with bay leaves and dill. Simply wrap in a piece of cheesecloth and add to the tub while the water is running. Keep a bouquet of fresh parsley, basil, and rosemary in a vase when working with spirits to repel any negative energies you might meet with.

PEANUT

In 1971 astronaut Alan Shepard took a peanut to the moon during his *Apollo 14* mission.

Form: raw, roasted, peanut butter, oil

Ruler: Jupiter

Element: Earth

Gods: Babalu-Aye, Ganesha

Goddesses: Erzulie Fréda, Lakshmi

Attributes: luck, prosperity

Culinary uses: The most obvious adaptation of peanuts is as peanut butter, which can be spread on sandwiches, act as an ice cream topper, or be the base for a variety of sauces (most notably pad thai). Chopped nuts can be a topping for stir-fries, add crunch to salads, or act as an ingredient in various forms of candy. Peanut oil has a mild flavor and a high smoke point, making it perfect for sautéing and pan-frying.

Magical uses: Leave peanuts on your altar as an offering to Ganesha when you'd like to change your luck. Save peanut shells to burn in a bonfire during prosperity rituals. Eat wheat toast with peanut butter and blackberry jam (or orange marmalade) before asking for a raise.

PEPPERMINT

Peppermint is easily (and cheaply) available at your local grocery store in tea bags. It can also often be found fresh in the produce aisle.

Form: fresh, dried, naturally flavored candies, extract

Ruler: Mercury

Element: Fire

Gods: Ellegua, Pluto

Goddesses: Hecate, Juno, Minthe

Attributes: anger management, health/healing, hex breaking, house cleansing, love, mental clarity, money draw, purification, renewal, strengthen psychic abilities, unblocking

Culinary uses: Add to hot or cold teas. Add a few fresh leaves to a jar of sugar. Let set for a week, remove leaves. Use peppermint sugar to lightly flavor teas, cookies, or brownies.

Magical uses: Add a pinch of peppermint to sleep pillows to help bring prophetic dreams. Burn peppermint when practicing divination or while studying. Use several peppermint stems to sprinkle blessed water around your home during house blessings to cleanse and send away any negative energies.

POPPY SEED

Poppies were offerings to the dead in both Greek and Roman myths.

Form: dried, paste

Ruler: Moon

Element: Water

God: Hypnos

Goddesses: Ceres, Demeter, Poppy Goddess

Attributes: ancestor offering, fertility, prophetic dreams, relaxation, restful sleep

Culinary uses: Poppy seeds can top a variety of baked goods or work sprinkled onto fruit salads. Poppy seed paste is the traditional filling for pastries during the Jewish holiday of Purim.

Magical uses: Add poppy seeds to dream or sleep pillows, or burn on self-lighting charcoal before bed to enhance psychic dreams. Bake poppy seed cakes to leave out during Samhain to honor your ancestors.

POTATO

In author Terry Pratchett's Discworld series, he writes of the "Potato Cult," with its patron deity of potatoes, Epidity.

Form: raw, cooked, instant flakes

Ruler: Moon

Element: Earth

Gods: none noted

Goddess: Axomama (Potato Mother)

Attributes: compassion, grounding, protection

Culinary uses: Bake, boil, mash, add to casseroles, shred for hash browns, toss into soups or stews. Instant flakes thicken sauces or soups.

Magical uses: Carve large potatoes into a poppet figure to represent someone whom you'd like to be more compassionate toward you. If possible, leave the poppet on the edge of their property. Mix instant potato flakes with black pepper, dried mustard, dill, and cumin. Sprinkle around your property to form a protective barrier against all negative energies.

RASPBERRY

According to Greek mythology, raspberries were once a white fruit, but were stained by the blood of Zeus's nursemaid Ida when she pricked her finger while picking the fruit.

Form: fresh, frozen, jelly

Ruler: Venus

Element: Moon

God: Zeus

Goddesses: Brighid, Huitaca

Attributes: fertility, love, strengthens romantic commitments

Culinary uses: Eat from your hand or mixed with cereal, yogurt, or ice cream. Add to fruit or green salads. Use to create rich sauces (both sweet and savory), jam, or a topping for pancakes and waffles.

Magical uses: Establish a tradition of serving raspberries on your romantic anniversaries as a magical way to strengthen your romantic bonds. Eat raspberries during any magical works when trying to become pregnant.

RICE

In the Luzon region of the Philippines, a carved wooden figure called a "bulul" is set out to guard the rice crops. It is thought to be given powers from the ancestral spirits of the property owners. Besides watching over rice crops, the bulul is also used in healing ceremonies.

Form: dried, instant, frozen

Ruler: Sun

Element: Air

Gods: Agathos, Buddha, Daimon, Ganesha

Goddesses: Dewi Sri, Gauri, Inari, Ivenopae, Mae Posop

Attributes: anxiety management, fertility, prosperity, protection, protection from ghosts, weather magic

Culinary uses: Rice is eaten the world over. From a breakfast cereal to sweet rice pudding and from casseroles to stir-fries, the culinary uses of rice are innumerable.

Magical uses: Carry rice for protection. When children leave the house, throw a few grains of rice after them (or sprinkle them in their backpack) to keep them safe on their daily travels. Use rice flour in floor sweeps for protection. Many spirits reportedly cannot leave grains of rice uncounted. If you are having unexplained and bothersome activity in your home, leave a bowl of rice out to keep the spirit busy and out of your hair. Throwing rice in the air is said to bring rain.

ROSEMARY

When the Greek goddess Aphrodite rose from the sea, legend has it that she was draped in rosemary. The name *rosemary* comes from the Latin "ros marinus," which means "dew of the sea."

Form: fresh, dried

Ruler: Sun

Element: Air

God: Ellegua

Goddesses: Aphrodite, Hebe, Mary, Venus

Attributes: banishment, brings feelings of comfort to the dead, cleansing, communication, courage, enhancement of psychic dreams, exorcism, fidelity, friendship, hex breaking, love, memory retention, mental clarity, nightmare prevention, protection, purification, travel protection

Culinary uses: Rosemary flavors chicken, lamb, pork, potatoes, rice, eggs, hash.

Magical uses: Honor those who have passed on and bring them comfort by sprinkling rosemary onto their final resting place. Burn dried rosemary on a charcoal block before bed to help prevent nightmares. In magical formulas, rosemary can substitute for almost any nontoxic herb. It is an especially good replacement for pine needles.

RYE

It was once thought that you could save yourself from a werewolf attack by running into a field of rye.

Form: flour, bread

Ruler: Venus

Element: Earth

Gods: Rongoteus

Goddesses: Demeter, Freya, Poludnitsa Zemyna, Zytnia Matka (Rye Mother)

Attributes: communication, humor, love, strengthens family bonds

Culinary uses: Rye flours create various types of breads.

Magical uses: Serve rye bread at family meals or during social gatherings to strengthen bonds of friendship and bring a sense of humor to a situation.

SAGE (CULINARY SAGE)

Though white sage has become a popular tool in magical cleansings and purification work, culinary or "common" sage has many of the same properties.

Form: fresh, dried

Ruler: Jupiter

Element: Air

Gods: Obatala, Zeus

Goddess: Maya

Attributes: anxiety management, business success, cleansing, healing, house blessings, hunting (think bargains!), money draw, prosperity, protection, purification, wisdom

Culinary uses: Flavor cheese, bread stuffings, sausages, veal, or liver with sage.

Magical uses: Add a tablespoon of dried sage to a small pot and pour two cups of boiling water over it. Let it sit for ten minutes, strain it, and add it to your cleaning water to help dispel negative energy in your home. Place a bit of dried sage in your wallet before you go out shopping for a good deal. Sage substitutes for mistletoe, sweetgrass, or white sage in any magical formula.

SALT

In ancient China salt would be burned and the ashes read as a type of divination. Divination by salt is called "alomancy."

Form: sea salt, kosher, Epsom

Ruler: Venus

Element: Water

Gods: Djamar, Huixtocihuatl, Kane, Kingu, Misor, Poseidon

Goddesses: Aphrodite, Astarte, Salacia, Salt Woman, Tiamat, Venus, Yemaya

Attributes: cleansing, exorcism, prosperity, protection

Culinary uses: Salt can be put into virtually anything.

Magical uses: Add salts to cleansing baths or floor sweeps to rid yourself or your home of negative energies. Salt forms the outline of protective circles, or you can draw protective symbols in salt.

SEAWEED

The most easily accessible form of seaweed might be nori, which will be in the Asian foods or international aisle of your grocery store. Nori is tenderer than other seaweeds.

Form: dried sheets

Ruler: Moon

Element: Water

Gods: Maui, Neptune, Poseidon

Goddesses: Benten, Hine-Nui-Te-Po, Yemaya

Attributes: brings feeling of joy; business success; money draw; protection of sailors, swimmers, or fishermen; strengthens psychic ability

Culinary uses: Nori can be used to wrap fish, rice, and vegetables. Nori can also be diced and added as a topping to soup or salads.

Magical uses: Add nori to floor sweeps for businesses success and to draw paying customers. Grind nori and sprinkle a bit in the corners of a room to encourage joyful feelings. Nori can be substituted in magical formulas calling for dulse or bladderwrack.

SESAME SEED/OIL

In Assyrian myth, the gods drank wine made from sesame seeds before they created the earth.

Form: oil, seeds

Ruler: Sun

Element: Fire

God: Ganesha

Goddess: Hecate

Attributes: fertility, justice, lust, nightmare prevention, prosperity for the household, road opener, truth

Culinary uses: Sesame seeds can top bagels or breads. Sesame oil flavors many Asian recipes and sauces.

Magical uses: Add a drizzle of sesame oil and/or sesame seeds over cooked fried rice that includes scrambled eggs for a triple whammy of fertility energy! If you are working a spell to get justice in a situation in which you've been wronged, dress the candle with sesame oil. Keeping an open jar of sesame seeds in your home is said to bring prosperity to the household.

SOY

During the Civil War, when true coffee was scarce, soldiers would brew "coffee" from soybeans.

Form: edamame, milk, miso, tofu, soy sauce

Ruler: Moon

Element: Water

God: Hou Tsi

Goddesses: Amaterasu, Ogetsu, Toyo-Uke-Bime, Ukemochi

Attributes: employment, luck, protection, psychic abilities

Culinary uses: Eat raw edamame as is or add to salads. Cooked, they can be added to a variety of stir-fries, casseroles, or soups. Tofu can function as a meat substitute, added to smoothies, soups, baked, fried, or put in stir-fries. The possibilities for this versatile food are almost endless.

Magical uses: Carry soybeans for luck. Eat soy (including soy sauce) for protection and to increase your psychic abilities. Drinking soy milk can help lead to successful employment.

SPEARMINT

Folklore states that you should not cut mint with a knife made of iron. This would seem to imply that mint was considered to be sacred to the fae.

Form: fresh, dried

Ruler: Mercury

Element: Air

God: Pluto

Goddess: Minthe

Attributes: enhances psychic dreams, happiness, memory retention, mental clarity, purification

Culinary uses: In British cooking, spearmint is sometimes added to flavor potatoes or peas. Spearmint also makes a flavorful tea.

Magical uses: Inhale the scent of spearmint to feel refreshed and invigorated. Drink spearmint tea while studying to increase information retention. You can find spearmint in tea bag form at your local grocer.

STAR ANISE

Though anise seed and star anise have similar flavors and similar names, they come from two very different plants. Many consider them to be interchangeable in magic, though I personally prefer star anise when it's available.

Form: dried

Ruler: Jupiter

Element: Air

Gods: none noted

Goddess: Oya

Attributes: purification, rebirth, strengthens psychic ability, wish magic

Culinary uses: Star anise is found in Chinese cuisine, used in sweets or with meat, poultry, soups, and stocks. It can flavor teas or mulled cider or wine.

Magical uses: Add star anise to simmering potpourri when performing divination to help increase intuition. Burn whole stars on charcoal blocks when working wish magic.

SUGAR

Sugarcane first came into the lexicon of Europe when Alexander the Great invaded India in 327 BC. It was reported back that "a remarkable kind of reed growing in India produced a kind of honey without the assistance of bees."

Form: cubes, loose, brown, white, simple syrups

Ruler: Venus

Element: Water

Gods: Cupid, Eros, Ganesha, Kamadeva, Tahatoi

Goddesses: Aphrodite, Kamakshi, Kateapiairiroro, Venus

Attributes: love

Culinary uses: Sugar sweetens almost anything.

Magical uses: Sugar can also "sweeten" a person's attitude toward you or a situation when you create a sugar jar. Write the person's name and/or details about a situation on a piece of paper. Place the paper in a small jar and cover completely with sugar. Add a lid and place the jar somewhere dark and quiet. Alternately, anoint a red taper candle with a bit of vanilla extract, then roll it in a mix of cinnamon and sugar for an instant love spell.

TAMARIND

Many Americans aren't very familiar with the taste of tamarind. Check out the international food aisle of your local grocery store to see if they carry one of the Mexican soft drink brands that produce tamarind soda (*tamarindo*).

Form: frozen, dried, paste, powder

Ruler: Saturn

Element: Water

Gods: Brahma, Krishna, Vishnu

Goddesses: Erzulie, Mariyamman, Ochun, Usha, Venus

Attributes: community bonds, friendship, lust

Culinary uses: Tamarind goes into drinks, baked goods, chutney, or seafood or poultry. Be careful not to overindulge, as it is also a natural laxative!

Magical uses: Serve your favorite tamarind recipe or tamarind soda at community events to help strengthen the bonds of friendship.

TARRAGON

Tarragon's scientific name is *Artemisia dracunculus,* and it is referred to as "dragon herb" or "dragonwort."

Form: fresh, dried

Ruler: Venus

Element: Earth

Gods: Tages, Tlaloc

Goddess: Artemis

Attributes: communication, hunting (think bargains!), luck

Culinary uses: Tarragon flavors poultry, chicken salad, mushrooms, tomatoes, or roasted fish.

Magical uses: Carry a sprig of fresh tarragon with you when taking an oral exam or when you have to make a speech to bring you luck and to help get your point across. Burn to commune with dragon spirits.

THYME

Folklore of the past states the belief that departed souls entered thyme flowers after death. Ancient Greeks placed thyme in the coffins of loved ones, while ancient Egyptians used it in mummification.

Form: fresh, dried

Ruler: Venus

Element: Water

God: Ares

Goddesses: Aphrodite, Freya

Attributes: aids in divinatory practices, attraction magic, cleansing, communication, draws fairies, health/healing, love, lust, nightmare prevention, purification, restful sleep, strengthens psychic abilities

Culinary uses: Add to give flavor to poultry, potatoes, veggies, eggs, bread stuffings, marinades for meat, seafood, cheese.

Magical uses: Add fresh thyme to a bath before going out to help attract a love interest. Grow thyme in your garden to attract fairies. Add a sprig of thyme to a vase of water when practicing divination to help open up your psychic abilities.

WALNUT

Roman grooms threw walnuts to the guests at their weddings as both a sign of their passage into manhood and as a blessing of good health and fertility to those gathered.

Form: fresh, shelled, oil

Ruler: Earth

Element: Earth

God: Jupiter

Goddess: Carya

Attributes: fertility, memory retention, protection

Culinary uses: Walnuts can be ground to make nut butter, used in baked goods or to top hot cereal, or sprinkled in green or fruit salads.

Magical uses: Carry a walnut in your pocket when you are studying for an exam to help retain the information. Carry the same walnut on the day of the test. Add ground walnut to fertility charms. Bury a walnut at each corner of your property for protection.

WHEAT

The word *cereal* comes from the name of the goddess Ceres, who watches over all types of grains, including wheat.

Form: flour, wheat germ, various hot and cold cereals

Ruler: Venus

Element: Earth

Gods: Bran, Min, Tammuz, Zeus

Goddesses: Cailleach, Ceres, Demeter, Ishtar, Isis, Onatha

Attributes: fertility, offering when giving thanks, prosperity, protection

Culinary uses: Wheat goes into creating a variety of baked goods.

Magical uses: Grind dry wheat cereals to add to protection spells or incense. Eat wheat bread when trying to become pregnant, but save a piece of each slice to put on your altar as an overnight offering. In the morning put the offering outside to feed the local birds.

WINE

The earliest evidence of wine comes from Iran, where archaeologists uncovered six 7,000-year-old jars that held the remains of both fermented grapes and a preservative made from tree resin.

Form: red or white

Ruler: Moon

Element: Water

Gods: Adonis, Anu, Asclepius, Bacchus, Dionysus, Ra, Shesmu

Goddesses: Bibesia, Gestin, Hathor, Ishtar, Meditrina, Oenothea, Sura, Yemaya

Attributes: ancestor offerings, love, purification

Culinary uses: Wine flavors sauces, stews, Italian recipes, and tomato dishes.

Magical uses: Offer wine at your ancestor altar. Share a glass of mulled wine with your lover to cement the romantic bond between the two of you. Add a splash of red wine to your purification bath. Not only is it purifying, but many swear by red wine's ability to soften skin!

YEAST

Never borrow yeast, as this is said to be bad luck.

Form: brewer's yeast, liquid yeast, rapid rise

Ruler: Jupiter

Element: Earth

Gods: None noted directly, but deities for brewing or bread can be substituted.

Goddesses: None noted directly, but deities for brewing or bread can be substituted.

Attributes: growing ideas, growing your business, money draw, prosperity

Culinary uses: Yeast is crucial to a variety of baked goods.

Magical uses: Add a pinch of yeast to any magical spell meant to grow or expand your business, prosperity, or ideas. Keep a pinch of yeast in your change jar to help draw money to your household.

INSTANT MAGIC: USING PREPACKAGED SPICE MIXES

In your grocery store spice aisle, you're sure to find an array of spice or herb mixes. When you need a quick magical fix, reach for a jar of ready-mixed herbs to sprinkle across your doorway, dress a candle, stuff a poppet, or any number of works.

Adobo Seasoning Mix

Adobo is a traditional Mexican spice mix containing paprika, black pepper, onion powder, oregano, cumin, hot chilies, and garlic powder. Magical uses include protection, banishing, or hex breaking. Combine half a jar of adobo seasoning mix with two cups of corn flour. Sprinkle around the outside of your home to get rid of negative energies.

Apple Pie Spice

A combination of cinnamon, nutmeg, cloves, and cardamom, apple pie spice is the perfect mix for spicing things up with your partner! Dress a red candle in grapeseed or olive oil—avoiding the wick—and roll it in apple pie spice. Burn while spending time with your lover. Or sprinkle this mix over a self-lighting charcoal instead.

Cajun Seasoning Mix

Generally a blend of paprika, salt, black and white peppers, garlic, onion powder, thyme, and cayenne, Cajun seasoning is perfect for strong protection. Use this mix to form circles when doing important works. Sprinkle just a pinch in the shoes of someone who needs a little watching over.

Chili Powder

Made with salt, hot chilies, onion, oregano, and garlic, chili powder is great for keeping away illness. Leave out tiny bowls of chili powder—out of reach of pets and children—during cold and flu season to help ward off illness.

Chinese Five-Spice Powder

Chinese Five-Spice Powder is an amazing blend of star anise, fennel seed, cinnamon, hot peppers, cloves, ginger, and licorice root. This mix lends itself to several kinds of herbal magic, including love spells, spells for igniting passion, and even spells for retaining information.

Cinnamon Sugar

With sugar sweetening a person or situation and cinnamon speeding up a spell, the two work great together when you need to get someone on your side quickly. Serve cinnamon toast to someone who could use some convincing. Sprinkling a little of the mix where you know a person will walk might influence them to look more kindly on your situation.

Curry Powder

Curry powder recipes can vary greatly brand to brand, so it's helpful that the mix already has some traditional uses! Turn to curry powder for protection, memory retention, and fertility spells.

Montreal Steak Seasoning

A combination of paprika, black and red peppers, garlic, salt, onion, dill, and coriander, this spice mix contains many of the individual ingredients you'd need to protect yourself or your home from ghosts or other negative energies. Create four small cloth pouches, fill them with this blend, and hang one in each of the farthest corners of your home.

Pickling Spice

Pickling spice can contain a wide variety of herbs and spices, but most are a mix of mustard seed, coriander, black pepper, dill, fennel seed, celery seed, and bay leaf. This combination can be used for many different intents, such as protection from ghosts or luck, lust, and wish magic.

Pumpkin Pie Spice

Pumpkin pie spice is one of my all-time favorite blends. I usually carry a small container of this mixture of cinnamon, ground ginger, nutmeg, and allspice in my on-the-go kit to add to almost any spell to "speed it up." It's also a great blend for business ventures, money draw, and simple healing spells.

six

Simple Sabbats for the Busy Witch

Many modern Pagans and other nature-friendly folks follow the cycles of nature, commonly called the Wheel of the Year. Holy days or sabbats consist of the solstices, equinoxes, and the points in between. When I was a new witch, many years ago, most of the books I read only offered elaborate rituals to mark the sabbats. I was left with the feeling that if I could not pull off an entire ritual perfectly, I was surely not worthy of being a witch. So when I was too busy, too tired, or too broke to put something amazing together, I often ended up just skipping the whole thing, which only made me feel disconnected, frustrated, and even guilty.

As I grew as both a person and a witch, I learned to relax and see the sabbats as what they really are: a way to mark the passing of the seasons, rather than an imposition to put on a big show. While we all get a great deal of satisfaction in pulling out all the stops, there are other times when you need something a little simpler and much more flexible. This chapter is all about those easy ways to celebrate to get the whole family involved when you don't have much time and without breaking the bank.

For each sabbat, I've shared a super-short solo ritual you can use to honor and reflect on the season when you only have five minutes. There are also simple group rituals for sharing with friends and activities to engage your kids in the Wheel of the Year. Let go of those feelings that there is a "right" way to honor the changing of the seasons and deity, and allow yourself to enjoy the celebration on any scale!

SAMHAIN–OCTOBER 31

Though many look to October 31 as Halloween, Pagans from around the world call it Samhain (Sow-en), a time to remember their ancestors and to celebrate the start of a new year. This period is well suited to practicing divination, working on transitions of all sorts, candle magic, protection magic, and working with or contacting those who have passed on.

October is often one of the busiest months of the year in a Pagan household. The fun of Halloween, creating costumes for the family, school events, and getting the household and property ready for the coming cooler weather keep us hopping. Sometimes there are not enough hours in the day to breathe, much less to plan a way to honor the season. Here are a few simple ways to celebrate.

Ritual: 5 Minutes Alone

This simple Samhain ritual lets you honor those who came before. If you have a few extra moments, add your favorite form of divination and see what the coming year will bring!

Items Needed:

- Your ancestor altar
- Lighter or matches
- A glass of apple cider
- A small snack, such as gingersnaps or a sliced apple

1. Sit before your ancestor altar and take a few deep breaths. Think about those who have passed on—their struggles and how they've affected your life. Think about how blessed you were to have them in your life.

2. When you feel centered and ready, light the candle on your altar and say,

I light this candle in honor of Samhain and to recognize the changing season. I honor the Lord and Lady and my ancestors and give them thanks. On this night, when their spirits walk among us and magic is in the air, I ask my ancestors for their blessings and ask them to watch over my family and home. So mote it be.

3. Sit for a moment or two. Drink your cider and eat your snack, being sure to leave some on your offering plate. Let the candle burn for as long as you safely can.

◆ ◆ ◆

Small Group Ritual

This ritual is just the right length to do with a friend or two, your partner, or the whole family. Just gather round and share the time together.

Items Needed:

- A candle
- A lighter or matches
- Scraps of paper
- A pen or pencil for each participant
- Your cauldron or other heat-safe container
- Cider and cups
- A plate of cookies

1. Gather everyone, and sit down somewhere comfortable with all of your ritual items. Begin with a simple deep breathing exercise to get everyone centered.

2. When everyone's ready, light the candle and say,

On this fall night of Samhain, we celebrate the turning wheel. As the seasons change, so goes the cycle of death and rebirth. Tonight we mark the death of the old year and the birth of the new. We make these pledges to ourselves and to the Lord and Lady.

3. At this time, each person should write down any resolutions that they'd like to make for the new year or any plans for new beginnings that they'd like to put into motion.

4. Go around the circle, and one at a time each participant can choose whether to share what they've written out loud. The paper is then lit on the flame of the candle (younger participants should be assisted by an adult) and placed in the cauldron to burn.

5. When everyone has finished, pass around the cider and cookies and enjoy each other's company. Everyone should save a sip of the cider and a bit of his or her cookie. When it's time to finish up, take the cooled ashes outside and bury them in the ground. Leave your food offerings nearby.

◆ ◆ ◆

For the Kids

There are usually more than enough Halloween activities going on in October for the kids. But how do you get them to understand what Samhain is really about? Create something fun to draw their attention while you count down the days!

Grab some orange construction paper and cut out thirty-one pumpkin shapes; number them 1 to 31 on one side. On the other side, write a short fact about Samhain, or paste on a picture of a loved one who's passed or share a fun fact about that person. If you like, staple or tape a small treat to each pumpkin, such as a piece of candy, a coin, a small Halloween eraser, or something like that. Starting on October 1, find a place to stash the pumpkin where you know your child will find it. Pack it in their school lunch, stick it in their sock drawer, or prop it up by their toothbrush. On Halloween morning, tape the last paper pumpkin to a real pumpkin and help them carve a face in it so that it can guard your home that night.

YULE—ON OR NEAR DECEMBER 21

Yule, which takes place every year on the winter solstice, is the shortest day of the year. Though Yule marks the official beginning of winter, it is also the time when the days begin to grow longer. Many traditions consider this time to be the rebirth of the sun and a celebration of light.

Ritual: 5 Minutes Alone

Yule may well be one of the busiest times of the year. It will only take a few minutes to perform this simple ritual of thanks to honor the season.

Items Needed:

- A red candle (Bayberry candles are traditionally said to bring warmth and wealth when lit on the solstice.)
- A lighter or matches
- A gingerbread cookie (or another holiday treat)
- Apple cider

1. Sit and center yourself when you have a few spare minutes. No matter what your spiritual practices, this time of the year is usually one of bustling families. Think about what this sabbat really means to you, and how you can better convey that message to your kids to make this day more special.

2. Light the candle and say,

   I light this candle in honor of the winter solstice and the return of the sun! I honor this celebration of light and welcome the lengthening of the days to come. I give thanks to the Lord and Lady for this change of the season and for the blessings bestowed upon my family. Blessed be.

3. Eat your treat and sit as long as you can, enjoying the time.

◆ ◆ ◆

Small Group Ritual

Many traditions hold that you should stay up on the night of the winter solstice to greet the return of the sun. Gather friends and family and plan an evening of fun to keep everyone awake until dawn. Depending on the crowd, this could be anything from an evening of video games to a marathon candle making night. What matters most is that you are enjoying each other's company.

Items Needed:

- A red candle for each participant
- A lighter or matches for each participant
- Enough small snacks to get through a long evening
- A pot of mulled apple cider or coffee

1. Before the evening starts, find out what time the sun will rise, and make sure to tell everyone you want to attend.

2. Spend the dark hours engaged in whatever activities you've devised to pass the time with enough small snacks and apple cider or coffee to see you through until dawn.

3. As the sun rises, have everyone light their candle. Have someone say,

We greet the sun on this day, the winter solstice! We ask that all who gather here be blessed, and that on these coming lengthening days, we gather often to enjoy each other's company.

4. Have everyone carefully hold up their candles and say together,

Welcome, Sun!

◆ ◆ ◆

For the Kids

This time of year, children can often be swept up by the commercial aspect of the holiday season. Make sure to share with them often that Yule is a celebration of light and the return of the sun and not just about presents. Many families do include gift giving as part of the winter holiday, so creating an atmosphere that makes giving just as exciting as getting can help curb any "gimme" attitudes. Consider participating in a local "Giving Tree," in which you fulfill a child's holiday wish, or "Mitten Tree," where you donate mittens, scarves, and hats. Partner up with other families and approach a local hospital or nursing home about having the kids create simple decorations to display. Make paper snowflakes, drawings, and holiday cards, and deliver them with some homemade treats to share with those who can't be home for the holiday. Creating a tradition of giving with your children will be one of the greatest gifts you will ever give them.

IMBOLC—FEBRUARY 1 OR 2

Imbolc (pronounced "Em-bulk"), or St. Brigid's Day, is a Celtic festival marking the beginning of spring. It is a time of rejuvenation, new beginnings, and purification. The word *imbolc* is thought to come from the Gaelic word *oimelc*, meaning "ewe's milk"; and the time of Imbolc was associated with sheep beginning lactation in preparation for the birth of their spring babies.

Many modern Pagans celebrate Imbolc as a fire festival honoring the goddess Brighid. As a domestic witch, I use this time to start planning my garden and order any seeds I might need for spring planting. It's also a great time of year to do a little love magic with your partner!

Ritual: 5 Minutes Alone

Imbolc is the perfect time for new beginnings. Use this ritual to help gather your thoughts on something new you'll be planning or participating in. Not only will it help you organize your ideas, but by declaring your intent, you'll start off your plans on a positive note!

Items Needed:

- A white or silver candle
- A lighter or matches
- A pen or pencil
- A piece of paper or your journal
- A small glass of milk (a traditional Imbolc beverage)

1. Take a moment to center yourself by taking a few deep breaths. Sit for a moment, reflecting on what this Imbolc means to you. Will you be working toward a new beginning in your life? Rejuvenating some aspect of a relationship? Removing or cleansing something in your life that is negative or cluttered? How are those resolutions you made back at Samhain coming along?

2. When you feel ready, light your candle and say,

   I light this candle in honor of Imbolc and to recognize the changing seasons. I honor the Lord and Lady and give them thanks as we travel ever closer to the spring.

3. With your goal for this season in mind, consider for a moment what actions you might take to further it; write down the steps you come up with. If you are planning a new beginning in the form of a new job, for example, you might write about updating your résumé, gathering applications, renewing old contacts, or taking a class to update your skills. If your goal is to cleanse your home of all clutter, write down the things you'll need to do so, such as gathering boxes for sorting or storage and separating things for donation, to throw away, or to recycle.

4. After you've put down your ideas and feel confident that you have a list that can help you move forward on your objectives, ask for the gods' and goddesses' aid in manifesting your aim and thank them for their help. Create a prayer yourself, or say,

Lord and Lady, as we move forward on the wheel of the year and move ever closer to spring, I ask for your help in manifesting my plans for this season.

5. Speak out loud about your goals and what you've planned to accomplish them, and then say,

As I work toward these goals, and as we travel toward the spring, I ask that you help me stay focused, move forward, and remember to honor you, myself, and my family while I do so.

6. Spend a bit of time, if you like, adding details to your plan, or just sitting in meditation on the season. When you are ready, take a drink of milk in honor of the season and extinguish your candle. The rest of the milk can be poured outside as an offering.

◆ ◆ ◆

Small Group Ritual

The same ritual as outlined above can be performed as a group ritual. Make its focus a communal project, such as planning a family vacation and the steps everyone will need to take to be able to afford it. Pagan friends might focus on expanding their group or finding a way to support their community.

◆ ◆ ◆

For the Kids

In Gaelic folklore, Imbolc is the time that Cailleach gathers her firewood for the rest of the winter. Since she doesn't want to stay out in bad weather gathering wood for a long winter, tradition says that good weather on Imbolc is a sign of more winter to come. And bad weather is a sign that an early spring is on its way.

Two or three weeks before Imbolc, discuss weather divination and rhymes with the kids. Give each child a piece of poster board with a grid for the days leading up to Imbolc (or with younger kids, use one piece and do the work together) and let them make weather predictions for each day based on what they have learned. On Imbolc, have everyone guess whether winter will stay longer or if spring is just around the corner. Here are a few old rhymes to get you started:

Red sky at night, sailor's delight.
Red sky at morning, sailor take warning.

Dry particles in the air tend to make the sky look red. If the western sky is red, the next day's weather tends to be dry. If the eastern sky is red in the morning, wet weather is headed your way.

Circle round the moon, rain or snow soon.

When it looks like there's a "circle" around the moon, this indicates that there is moisture in the air, which often brings precipitation of some sort.

If the sun shines bright on Candlemas Day
The half of the winter's not yet away.

Another predictor that if there is good weather on Imbolc (also known by some as "Candlemas"), the end of winter is still far off. If you have a pine tree nearby, check out the pinecones. If they are closed, it's said that wet weather is on the way. Open cones mean dry weather.

OSTARA (SPRING EQUINOX)—
ON OR ABOUT MARCH 20

Ostara is a time of beginnings, growth, and the first day of spring! Unlike most of the other modern sabbats, Ostara is not based on Celtic tradition, but instead comes to us from Germany. According to the Venerable Bede, in his book *De temporum ratione* (*The Reckoning of Time*) written in the year 725, this holiday is named after the German fertility goddess Eostre. Ostara is the time to work on fertility magic, communication, growth, love, sex, and adding more balance to your life. It's also a great time to bless those seeds that you might have ordered at Imbolc!

Ritual: 5 Minutes Alone

This Ostara ritual is geared toward reaffirming the goals you set at Imbolc and helping them to continue blossoming through this season of growth.

Items Needed:

- Enough dirt or potting soil to hold a candle securely (soil from your yard is best)
- A heatproof container to hold dirt and a candle
- A candle in your favorite spring color, shape, or scent
- A lighter or matches

1. Place the soil in the container.

2. Place the candle in the dirt, making sure that it is stable and secure.

3. Sit for a few moments and center yourself. Think of the coming spring and what things you need to grow or renew in your life. Still working on your goals from Imbolc? Looking to learn a new skill or start a new project? When you are ready, light the candle and say the following words (or words you've written yourself):

I light this candle in honor of Ostara, the spring equinox! I honor the changing of the seasons, and the reawakening of the earth. With spring comes lighter days, warmth, and the beginnings of new growth. With spring comes my vow to work to grow and expand my plans and goals. I give thanks to the Lord and Lady for their blessings, and ask them to be with me as I continue on my path. So mote it be!

4. Snuff out your candle, but leave it resting on your Ostara or family altar.

5. Throughout the spring season, relight the candle when you are working toward your goals or when you need a bit of inspiration or encouragement.

◆ ◆ ◆

Small Group Ritual

This is a simple craft idea for a group of older children or adults. My coven has enjoyed doing this activity for several years, and we always have great fun seeing what kinds of patterns and symbols everyone comes up with!

Items Needed:

- 4 blown-out eggs per person[1]
- A white crayon
- An egg dyeing kit or a selection of natural egg dyes. If time is limited, these can be made ahead of time. (See pages 155–156 for instructions on natural dyes from the kitchen.)
- Small squares of tissue paper in various colors
- A package of white birthday candles
- A small funnel
- A variety of herbs (see chart on page 154)
- A candle in your favorite spring color, shape, or scent
- A lighter or matches
- Lemonade
- A seasonal food to share such as deviled eggs, chocolates, or something made with early March veggies such as avocados or asparagus

---

1 To blow out eggs: Rinse your batch of eggs well in cool water. Select an egg, and drill a small hole at each end of the shell using a nail. Holding the egg over a bowl, blow into the egg so that the insides come out of the opposite hole and drain into the bowl. Rinse the eggshell and set it back into the carton. Repeat with the rest of the eggs. Let the carton sit for a day or two to make sure the eggshells are thoroughly dried. Use the insides of your eggs to make scrambled eggs or an omelet.

	Prosperity	Love	Protection	Healing
Color	Gold or green	Pink, blue-green	Gold, purple	Pale blue, green
Herbs	Basil, bay leaf, chamomile, cinnamon, parsley, pine, wheat	Basil, catnip, chamomile, cinnamon, clove, dill, ginger, nutmeg, peppermint, rosemary, spearmint, thyme	Basil, bay leaf, cinnamon, dill, garlic, mint, mustard, parsley, pepper, pine, rose, rosemary, sage	Barley, bay leaf, cinnamon, dill, ginseng, flax, mint, oregano, pine, peppermint, sage, thyme

1. Gather everyone around a table where all your work items have been set out. If there is anyone attending who isn't familiar with Ostara, explain what the sabbat is about and share with everyone that you'll be making magic Ostara eggs.

2. Give everyone their eggs and a copy of the chart below. Using a white crayon, draw words or symbols that represent Ostara to you on the eggs (the colored area won't take the dye).

3. Color the eggs and set aside to dry for a few minutes.

4. Taking a small piece of tissue paper, cover one of the holes of each egg.

5. Light a birthday candle and allow the wax to drip over the edges of the paper to seal them to the egg.

6. When the wax has hardened, use the funnel to add a pinch of whichever herbs have been chosen.

7. Seal the open end as you did the first.

8. When everyone has finished dyeing, filling, and sealing up his or her eggs, light the candle and say,

We light this candle in honor of Ostara, the spring equinox! We honor the changing of the seasons and the reawakening of the earth. As the land warms and blossoms, we ask that these things in our lives also blossom and grow: prosperity, love, protection, and healing! May the Lord and Lady bless these magical eggs we have created together!

9. Let the candle continue to burn as you enjoy each other's company and your small feast. Save a bit of food and drink to place outside as an offering. Each guest should take their decorated eggs home with them, to be buried in their garden or a pot of soil along with a few seeds, so the wishes for prosperity, love, protection, and healing can grow alongside the new plants.

◆ ◆ ◆

For the Kids

Get out your pots and pans and create some natural egg dyes using this simple recipe. Take the time to explain that eggs are a symbol of the goddess of spring and how using natural dyes on the eggs instead of store-bought color kits brings us closer to nature.

Basic Dye Recipe

Coloring your eggs with natural items found in your kitchen is not only fun, but a lesson for the kids on cooking, chemical changes, and the art and magic of color. Follow the basic directions below, adding the natural ingredients to get just the right color.

Items Needed:

- 3 cups hot water
- Natural dye (see color options and ingredients below)
- Pinch of salt
- 2 tablespoons white vinegar
- 1 tablespoon cream of tartar
- Hard-boiled eggs

1. Bring the water to a boil.

2. Add your dye ingredient from the list below (about half a cup of the fresh ingredient, or 1 tablespoon of the dried).

3. Simmer for 15 minutes, stirring occasionally.

4. Strain the colored liquid and return it to the pan. If you'd like a deeper, darker color, repeat these steps.

5. When you are satisfied with the color of your dye, add the salt, white vinegar, and cream of tartar to the pan. Mix well and allow to cool slightly.

6. Add the hard-boiled eggs and allow them to sit until they reach your desired color.

- **Green** (growth, prosperity, healing, fertility): spinach, fresh parsley, grass (only if it has not been chemically treated), green onion tops

- **Red** (love, lust, marriage) or pink (friendship, emotional healing, innocent romance): blackberries, cranberry or pomegranate juice, strawberries

- **Purple** (spiritual growth, tolerance, psychic development): beets, grape juice, hibiscus tea bags, red onion skins

- **Yellow** (new beginnings, creativity, happiness, luck, communication): carrot tops, celery leaves, peel from yellow or light green apples, chamomile tea bags, cumin

- **Brown** (animal magic, learning, home and hearth): walnut shells, the meat of acorns, coffee grounds, black tea, instant coffee granules

- **Blue** (peace, serenity, healing, loyalty, empathy): blueberries, red cabbage, beets

- **Orange** (power, energy, successful competition): chili powder, paprika, yellow onion skins

Alternately—though they are not exactly a natural ingredient—unsweetened powdered drink mix packets can be used instead of the plant material to create deeper colors without quite as much time or effort.

BELTANE (MAY DAY)—MAY 1

In ancient days, Beltane (literally "bright fire") was the time when animals were led back out to their summer feeding grounds. Baby animals, nests full of eggs, and plants starting to sprout mark this sabbat. As Samhain honors those who have passed, Beltane honors living and growing things. If you're trying to become pregnant, it is a time to work on fertility magic. Gardens and plants can be blessed to help bring an abundant harvest in the coming months. Wish magic and prosperity magic take advantage of the vibrations of fertility and abundance in early May as well.

Ritual: 5 Minutes Alone

The following ritual for Beltane simply honors the season and the fertile earth. If you are seeking to become pregnant, try changing the last half of the last line to, "for my womb to be as the earth: fertile and filled with life."

Items Needed:

- A candle in your favorite spring color or scent
- A lighter or matches

Ground and center yourself. Light your candle and say,

Today I light this candle to celebrate the joyful sabbat of Beltane! As the fertile earth bursts into bloom, I ask the Lord and Lady for my life to be as the earth: in full bloom and filled with joy and color. So mote it be!

◆ ◆ ◆

Small Group Ritual

Beltane is such a great sabbat to bring friends together. If the weather is accommodating, consider having a potluck or a barbecue before or after the ritual.

Items Needed:

- Lengths of yarn in bright colors
- A source of lively music

1. Gather friends and family outside around your favorite tree. Take turns loosely tying or just looping the lengths of yarn onto its branches while making silent wishes for things you hope to grow in your life this Beltane season.

2. When everyone is done, gather around (or just near if necessary) the tree and hold hands. Have someone say,

We gather together in joy to greet the Beltane season! We ask for blessings upon this fertile earth and for all gathered here. So mote it be!

3. Turn on the music and give in to joyful dancing!

4. Keep an eye on the tree for the birds that will come to carry off the yarn wishes to help build their nests.

For the Kids

The energy of fertility and growth makes Beltane the perfect time for wish magic. Use the recipe below to mix up a big batch of liquid bubbles. Take the kids outside on a warm day and have them whisper their hopes into the bubbles that will carry their words up to the Lord and Lady.

Liquid Bubbles

There's not much more fun to be had on a warm spring day than blowing bubbles and making wishes. This is my favorite bubble mixture recipe. It not only makes a large container of bubbles, but it's also very inexpensive.

Items Needed:

- 1 gallon cold water
- 1 cup dishwashing liquid

- ¼ cup corn syrup
- Optional: several drops liquid food coloring

Combine all ingredients and stir gently. Store unused mixture in a covered container.

LITHA (SUMMER SOLSTICE)—
ON OR ABOUT JUNE 21

The summer solstice marks the longest day of the year. The Litha season is a great time to recharge your magical tools, get handfasted, gather herbs for medicinal use, gather water from a running source for magical use, and, of course, to watch for the fae that are out and about!

Litha is second only to Samhain as my favorite sabbat! By June 21, my garden is usually in full swing, the kids are out of school, and we are enjoying lazy summer days of swimming, catching crabs off the local pier, or just sitting outside with a good book. Litha is perfect for diving into nature full throttle, spending days hiking in the woods, exploring the beach, finding a park to enjoy, or picnicking or grilling with family and friends.

Ritual: 5 Minutes Alone

By the time Litha rolls around, the weather is warm, the kids are out of school, and hopefully you're in full swing of enjoying the lazy days that are this season. Light up your candle and give thanks for the opportunity to spend time outside with those you love.

Items Needed:

- A red, orange, or gold candle
- A lighter and matches

1. Find a quiet corner to yourself with candle and lighter in hand.

2. Sit and give yourself a moment to settle, relax, and center. Breathe deeply in and out.

3. When you are ready, light the candle and say,

By lighting this candle, I honor the summer solstice. By fire, I honor the deities of the season, the earth, and the turning of the wheel. I thank you for the warm days and the lazy summer evenings spent with family and friends. May I remember to enjoy each and every moment spent together, and be thankful for the time we share. So mote it be!

• • •

Small Group Ritual

This group ritual is meant to reaffirm the bonds of friendship and the group's commitment to one another.

Items Needed:

- A white candle in a sturdy holder
- A red, orange, or gold taper candle for each person and an inexpensive holder for each or one larger-size pillar candle and one sturdy holder
- A carving tool (wooden toothpicks or skewers work great)
- A lighter or matches
- A pitcher of sun-brewed iced tea
- A bowl of summer fruits

1. Gather everyone together outside and lead them through taking a few deep breaths to ground and center.

2. When everyone is ready, light the white candle and say,

We gather under the sun with friends and family to celebrate Litha! Lord and Lady, please bless those who gather here to pay tribute to you and the summer season.

3. If the group gathered is family or a group that spends time together on a regular basis, instead of carving individual candles, find one larger-sized pillar candle and have everyone take turns carving into it. Light the candle each time the group gathers during the Litha season, or if it's

a family candle, light it each night at dinnertime or in the evening when you're winding down from your day. If the group is less familiar, pass out the candles and carving tools. Have everyone carve into them symbols, runes, or sigils that represent the Litha season to them.

4. When everyone is done carving, say,

Lord and Lady, bless these candles and know them as a symbol of this solar season. To light one is to give thanks for this glorious Litha season!

5. Have everyone light his or her individual candle from the wick of the white candle. When all the candles are lit, have everyone say,

So mote it be!

6. Set the candles in their holders and allow them to burn while you enjoy your food and drink together. Each person should take their candle home with them to light any time they are feeling the blessings of the summer.

◆ ◆ ◆

For the Kids

Summertime is when the fairies are out in force to enjoy the herbs and flowers in full bloom. On the full moon before the solstice, give each child a small jar. Let them fill it with fresh thyme, cover the thyme with olive oil, and cap it off tightly. Every evening, the jar should be given a good shake. On the night before Litha, help them strain the oil into a clean jar and leave it overnight on the family altar.

Early on Litha, take the kids out for a walk to gather natural items to create a fairy house: twigs on the ground, interesting rocks, pinecones, acorns, or even shells if you live near enough to the water. Find an out-of-the-way spot in your yard or garden—or even a terra-cotta pot filled with potting soil that can sit by your door—and let the kids put everything together to create a fairy house. Save a flat rock or clamshell to sit out front of the house for offerings if you'd like. After the house has been completed, leave it undisturbed for the rest of the day. In the evening, when the sun starts to go down, and the fireflies start to come out, help the kids anoint their eyelids with a tiny swipe of their thyme oil to see if they might be able to catch any fairies dancing around their new home!

LAMMAS (LUGHNASADH)—AUGUST 1

Whether you call it Lammas, Lughnasadh, or something else, many Pagans celebrate this day as the halfway mark between Litha and Mabon. Traditionally, this is a harvest festival, particularly for grain. A simple way to celebrate the season is to bake and share your favorite bread recipe. Magically, Lammas is a good time to do works associated with protection of your home, health and healing, and prosperity. Many Pagans honor the sun god Lugh at this time and may create a corn "god" or loaf of bread in the shape of a man to ritually "sacrifice."

Ritual: 5 Minutes Alone

At this time when crops are traditionally fully grown and ready for harvesting, it's a good time to step back and count your blessings and give a bit of thanks for the prosperity your family has. If you aren't feeling very blessed, try to spend some time volunteering with those less fortunate. Sometimes we're more prosperous than we realize.

Items Needed:

- A gold, red, or orange candle
- A lighter or matches
- A piece of whole grain bread
- A yeasty beer or glass of apple juice

1. Set aside a few minutes for yourself. Begin by centering yourself. Take a few deep breaths, and light your candle as you say,

   This candle I light to honor Lammas and this time of harvest and abundance. I give thanks for the plenty of my family and ask for continued blessings for my family and for all living things upon this earth. So mote it be!

2. Drink and eat while you count your blessings.

◆ ◆ ◆

Small Group Ritual

This get-together is less a ritual than a coming together to share. It's a good way to remember that as long as you have a little extra to share, you're blessed.

Lammas is the perfect sabbat for a group to bake bread together. Share your blessings and abundance with friends on a baking day. Make enough bread for everyone to take home a loaf, plus plenty of extras to donate to a local food pantry, soup kitchen, or shelter. Before parting ways at the end of the day, make sure to share one of the loaves that you baked together and thank the God and Goddess for the time you shared.

◆ ◆ ◆

For the Kids

Create a "harvest collage" on a piece of poster board. Gather seeds, dried corn, dried corn husks, pictures of foods that will be harvested during the season, and representations of harvest deities. While you work on the collage together, talk about where foods come from and how important it is to care for the earth that supplies everything we need for life. When the collage is done, hang it over or near the family altar for display throughout the Lammas season.

MABON (FALL EQUINOX)— ON OR ABOUT SEPTEMBER 21

The autumn equinox marks the time when the days start growing shorter and the weather begins to cool. Mabon is the witch's day of thanksgiving: time to count your blessings and share them with others. Give thanks to deity for all you have in your life, to your friends and family for their support, and recognize your own hard work contributing to the successes in your life.

Ritual: 5 Minutes Alone

The fall season finds us creeping toward colder weather, and for some that means the winter blues. This simple ritual is for us to once again give thanks and remember what we are grateful for. Let those thoughts help sustain you through the months to come.

Items Needed:

- A candle in your favorite fall color or scent
- A lighter or matches
- A drink and a snack: Think fall! Apple cider or herbal tea along with leaf-shaped cookies, fresh bread, a pumpkin or apple muffin, or a crisp fall apple.

1. Gather your items and find a quiet place to sit.

2. Center yourself by taking a few deep, cleansing breaths.

3. Consider the season that is coming to pass and the abundance that you've received and the work you've done to obtain it.

4. Light the candle and say,

   I light this candle to honor the season and to give thanks for the abundance in my life. I strive to remember these blessings and give thanks for them throughout the entire year. I strive to remember to share those blessings with others not as fortunate as I am, even when I have little to share. I give thanks to the Lord and Lady for all my blessings this Mabon season, and give thanks for all those blessings that will come to me this glorious fall season. So mote it be!

5. Enjoy your snack; then leave the last sip of your drink and bite of your food outside as an offering.

◆ ◆ ◆

Small Group Ritual

Not only does this ritual work for Mabon, but if you're hosting a Thanksgiving dinner in November, it can be done again then!

Items Needed:

- A pen or pencil for each participant
- Small squares of paper

- A candle in your favorite fall color or scent
- A lighter or matches
- A drink and a snack: Think fall! Apple cider or herbal tea along with leaf-shaped cookies, fresh bread, a pumpkin or apple muffin, or a crisp fall apple
- Your cauldron or heat-safe container

1. Guide your group through a short deep breathing exercise of meditation.

2. When everyone is relaxed and centered, pass out the paper and writing tools and have everyone write down what they are grateful for this season or a few words of thanks to the Lord and Lady.

3. Light the candle and say,

   We gather here today to honor the sacred day of Mabon. We give thanks to the Lord and Lady for this group of friends and family and for the blessings we have all received throughout this year.

4. Share what you have written on your papers. Each participant can then fold their paper in half and one at a time light them on the candle flame and drop them into the cauldron to send their thanks off to the universe.

5. Enjoy your drink and snack (saving a bit to go outside as an offering) and each other's company. When it's time to part, snuff out the candle and say,

   Till we gather again, may the blessings of the Lord and Lady be yours. So mote it be!

◆ ◆ ◆

For the Kids

Purchase a large piece of poster board and draw or paint a tree on it with many stretching branches. You can either do a family tree for everyone to use, or let each of your kids have one of their own that they can hang on their bedroom door. Using fall-colored construction paper, cut out leaf shapes (about forty per child). On Mabon, gather the kids around and tell them what Mabon is all about and share with them something that you are grateful for. Each child can then write or draw one thing for which they give thanks on a leaf and glue the leaf to the tree every day until Samhain.

Appendix I

Herbs and Foods Listed by Need

Addiction (overcoming; see also "Bad Habits"): bergamot

Ancestor Work/Appeases the Dead: apples, beans, chocolate, corn, honey, molasses, oats, orange, poppy seed, rosemary, wine

Anger Management: almond, basil, chamomile, peppermint

Anxiety Management: avocado, chamomile, rice, sage

Attraction: cloves, nutmeg, thyme

Bad Habits (overcoming): almond, bergamot

Banishment: basil, beets, black pepper, cumin, onion, rosemary

Business Success: allspice, basil, sage, seaweed, yeast

Clairvoyance: bay leaf

Cleansing/Clearing Negativity: baking soda, bay leaf, beer, chamomile, egg-shell, garlic, lemon, onion, orange peel, parsley, peppermint, rosemary, sage, salt, thyme

Communication: beans, caraway seed, cilantro, rosemary, rye, tarragon, thyme

Compassion: potato

Community (to strengthen bonds): tamarind

Confidence Booster: bergamot, orange

Courage: ginger, rosemary

Creativity: barley, basil, blackberries, chives, cilantro, cinnamon, coffee, dried beans, orange peel, yeast

Divination: anise, basil, bay leaf, nutmeg, thyme

Employment: alfalfa, allspice, bay leaf, buckwheat, cilantro, cinnamon, flaxseed, oats, soy milk

Energy Boosters (magical): apricot, asparagus, bergamot, coffee, ginger

Exorcism: basil, bay leaf, black pepper, dried beans, garlic, lemon, parsley, rosemary, salt

Fertility: almond, avocado, banana, barley, basil, bread, coconut, corn, dill, egg, eggshells, flaxseed, garlic, honey, mustard seed, parsley, poppy seed, raspberry, rice, sesame seed, walnut, wheat

Fidelity: anise, apple, basil, caraway seed, cinnamon, cumin, dill, ginger, parsley, raspberry, rosemary, rye, sesame seed

Friendship (to attract or strengthen): Brazil nut, dill, lemon, orange, rosemary, tamarind

Glamour: apple, orange

Gossip (to stop): cloves

Grounding: potato

Happiness/Joy: avocado, basil, chamomile, cloves, oregano, seaweed, spearmint

Healing (spiritual): fennel seed

Health/Healing: allspice, apricot, bay leaf, beer, cinnamon, fennel seed, flaxseed, garlic, ginger, honey, lemongrass, nutmeg, olive oil, orange, oregano, peppermint, sage, thyme

Heartbreak Ease: almond, apple, chives, cloves, marjoram

Hex Breaking: beer, black pepper, cayenne, crushed red pepper, dill, eggshells, peppermint, rosemary

House Blessing: basil, cabbage, flaxseed, olive oil, sage

Humor: rye

Hunting: apple, sage, tarragon

Justice: sesame seed

Love: alfalfa, almond, apple, avocado, barley, basil, beet, cardamom, cheese, chocolate, cinnamon, cloves, coffee, coriander, corn, cumin, dill, fennel seed, garlic, honey, lemon, lemongrass, marjoram, orange, oregano, parsley, peppermint, raspberry, rosemary, rye, sugar, thyme, wine

Luck: allspice, aloe vera, anise, basil, bay leaf, beans, ginger, honey, marjoram, nutmeg, olive oil, oregano, peanut, soy beans, tarragon

Lunar magic: lemon

Lust: anchovies, apple, apricot, artichoke, arugula, asparagus, avocado, basil, bay leaf, beans (dried), blackberries, caraway seed, cardamom, cayenne, chocolate, cinnamon, coriander, crushed red pepper, cumin, ginger, marjoram, mustard seed, nutmeg, olive oil, parsley, sesame seed, tamarind, thyme

Marriage (to strengthen): basil, raspberry

Meditation: chamomile

Mental Awareness/Clarity: caraway seed, cilantro, coriander, lemongrass, mustard seed, peppermint, rosemary, spearmint

Money Draw: allspice, avocado, basil, bay leaf, chamomile, cinnamon, ginger, molasses, nutmeg, oregano, peppermint, sage, seaweed, yeast

Motivation: chives

New Beginnings/Rebirth: egg, peppermint, star anise

Nightmare Prevention: anise, dried beans, rosemary, sesame seed, thyme

Obstacle Movers (unblocking): allspice, chives, coffee, peppermint

Personal Growth: artichoke, ginger

Prosperity: alfalfa, almond, asparagus, banana, barley (especially in business), basil, blackberry, Brazil nut, bread, buckwheat, butter, cabbage, cardamom, chamomile, cilantro, cloves, corn, fennel seed, flaxseed (especially in business), milk, molasses (for business), nutmeg, oats, olive oil, orange, peanut, rice, sage, salt, sesame seed, wheat, yeast

Protection: aloe vera (home), anise (for spiritual protection while sleeping), artichoke (physical and spiritual), asparagus, basil, bay leaf, beans, blackberries, black pepper, blueberries (from psychic attack), bread, broccoli (spiritual), brussels sprouts (spiritual), butter, cabbage, caraway seed, cayenne, chives, cinnamon, corn, crushed red pepper, cumin, dill (from ghosts), fennel seed, flaxseed (of children), garlic, lemon (during sleep), marjoram (of families), milk, mustard seed (from ghosts), olive oil, onion, parsley, potato, rice, rosemary, sage, salt, seaweed (of sailors, swimmers, and fishermen), soy sauce, walnut, wheat

Psychic Abilities (to block): dried beans

Psychic Abilities (to strengthen): bay leaf, cinnamon, lemongrass, nutmeg, peppermint, seaweed, soy (eating), star anise, thyme

Psychic Dreams (to enhance): bay leaf, chamomile, poppy seed, rosemary, spearmint

Purification: anise, bay leaf, cinnamon, coconut, lemon, lemongrass, milk, parsley, peppermint, rosemary, sage, spearmint, star anise, thyme, wine

Relaxation: beer, chamomile, rice, sage, poppy seeds

Remembrance (also see "Study Aids"): mustard seed, rosemary

Repel Illness: garlic

Road opener: coffee, sesame seed

Sleep: beer, chamomile, poppy seed, thyme

Stamina: asparagus, barley

Strength (physical): bay leaf, ginger

Study Aids/Memory Retention: bay leaf, bergamot, caraway seed, cloves, fennel seed, rosemary, spearmint, walnut

Success: arugula, cinnamon, cloves, ginger, orange

Thanks Giving: bread, wheat

Theft Prevention: caraway seed, cumin

Travel Protection: banana, basil (including for the dead), bergamot, fennel seed, rosemary

Weather Magic: dill, rice

Wisdom: bay leaf, caraway seed, sage

Wish Magic: bay leaf, beans, egg, star anise

Appendix II

Magical Use of Oils

While there are many more oils to choose from than the ones listed here, I've limited this list to oils that you can usually find in your local grocery store. Look in the cooking oil section, the medical aisle, and the skin/hair care aisle.

You can extend the shelf life of your oil when using it for magical purposes by adding 10 percent wheat germ, 10 percent jojoba oil, or a few drops of vitamin E oil. Check out chapter 5 for ready-made recipes using these oils.

ALMOND OIL

Element: Air

Gods: Attis, Chandra, Hermes, Jupiter, Liber Pater, Mercury, Obatala, Odin, Oko, Ptah, Thoth, Zeus

Goddesses: Artemis, Athena, Diana, Hecate, Ochun, Rhea, Yemaya

Culinary uses: Heat damages the flavor of nut oils; best used with uncooked or cold foods.

Magical uses: consecration of tools corresponding with Air, money draw, wisdom

Shelf life: 4–6 months

APRICOT KERNEL OIL

Element: Water

Gods: Oko, Shango

Goddesses: Ochun, Venus

Culinary uses: Apricot kernel oil is not frequently used for cooking because it tends to be expensive. It can be used as a salad oil. When using apricot kernel oil for cooking, make sure it's labeled as edible. Oil used for cosmetic purposes may have added stabilizers.

Magical uses: love, self-esteem, lust, consecration of tools corresponding with Water

Shelf life: 6 months–1 year. Refrigerate after opening.

AVOCADO OIL

Element: Water

God: Orion

Goddesses: Bast, Flora, Hathor

Culinary uses: Avocado oil has a very light flavor that is slightly nutty. It's perfect for salad dressings, and low in saturated fat, high in polyunsaturated.

Magical uses: lust, joyful feelings

Shelf life: up to 1 year

CANOLA OIL

Element: Fire

God: Asclepius

Goddess: Lakshmi

Culinary uses: Canola oil has a mild flavor and a high smoke point, making it a good oil for all-purpose cooking. It is one of the most inexpensive oils and has the least amount of saturated fat of any oil.

Magical uses: fertility, protection from ghosts

Shelf life: up to 1 year

CASTOR OIL

Element: Air

Gods: None noted

Goddess: Garbarakshambigai

Culinary uses: none noted

Magical uses: hex breaking, protection

Shelf life: 12–14 months

COCONUT OIL

Element: Water

Gods: Mars, Oko

Goddesses: Athena, Nut, Yemaya

Culinary uses: Heat stable, with a smoke point of 350 degrees. Good for both sautéing and baking, coconut oil does give a mild coconut flavor to recipes.

Magical uses: protection, cleansing, consecration of tools corresponding with Water

Shelf life: 1 year+

CORN OIL

Element: Earth

Gods: Adonis, Centeotl, Centzon Totochtin, Dionysus, Fast-ta-chee, Gwion, Ioskeha, Oko, Osiris, Xochipilli, Yum Caax

Goddesses: Ceres, Chicomecoatl, Corn Mother, Hecate, Isis, Iyatiku, Kornjunfer, Nepit, Onatha, Perigune, Selu, Xilonen, Yellow Woman

Culinary uses: Corn oil has almost no flavor and a high smoke point, making it a good all-purpose cooking oil. It is high in polyunsaturated fat.

Magical uses: prosperity, protection, love, fertility

Shelf life: 4–6 months

GRAPESEED OIL

Element: Water

Gods: Adonis, Asclepius, Bacchus, Dionysus, Liber Pater, Ra, Shesmu

Goddesses: Bibesia, Hathor, Meditrina, Sura, Yemaya

Culinary uses: A by-product of wine, this light oil is a good choice for salad dressings.

Magical uses: fertility, increase psychic abilities, money draw

Shelf life: 3–6 months

HAZELNUT OIL

Element: Fire

Gods: Aengus mac Og, Hermes, Mercury, Thor

Goddesses: Artemis, Diana, Ochun

Culinary uses: Best used on raw foods or drizzled over cooked foods right before serving. Also makes a good substitution for vegetable oils in most vinaigrette recipes.

Magical uses: luck, wish, magic, fertility, consecration of tools corresponding with Fire

Shelf life: Up to 3 months at room temperature, a bit longer if refrigerated, but it will solidify. Bring to room temperature before using.

JOJOBA OIL

Element: Water

God: Adonis

Goddesses: None noted

Culinary uses: None noted

Magical uses: Never becomes rancid. Mix with other oils for magical use to extend their shelf life. Substitute jojoba oil in any magical formulas that call for ambergris.

Shelf life: 1 year+

OLIVE OIL

Element: Fire

Gods: Apollo, Aristaeus, Brahma, Cupid, Eros, Hermes, Indra, Mars, Mercury, Pan, Poseidon, Ra, Wotan

Goddesses: Athena, Minerva

Culinary uses: Olive oil comes in a variety of flavors, depending on how the oil was extracted.

Magical uses: prosperity, fertility, fidelity, health/healing, success, rebirth

Shelf life: up to 1 year

PEANUT OIL

Element: Earth

God: Ganesha

Goddess: Babalu-Aye

Culinary uses: Mildly flavored, peanut oil has a high heat point and is great for deep-frying foods.

Magical uses: prosperity, luck

Shelf life: up to 1 year

SAFFLOWER OIL

Element: Fire

God: Shango

Goddess: Ochun

Culinary uses: Inexpensive and flavorless, this is a good oil for everything from salad dressings to light frying.

Magical uses: Safflower oil is magically neutral so it works for virtually anything.

Shelf life: 6 months

SESAME OIL

Element: Fire

God: Ganesha

Goddess: Hecate

Culinary uses: Used mainly in Indian and Asian recipes, sesame oil in its light form can be used for most types of cooking, including deep-frying. Dark sesame oil can be used for stir-frying, but its smoke point is not appropriate for deep frying.

Magical uses: lust, prosperity for the household, fertility, justice, nightmare prevention, road opener, truth

Shelf life: up to 1 year

SOYBEAN OIL

Element: Water

God: Hou Tsi

Goddesses: Amaterasu, Ogetsu, Toyo-Uke-Bime, Ukemochi

Culinary uses: Soybean oil's high smoke point makes it a good choice for frying or sautéing. Its neutral flavor is perfect for salad dressings or baked goods.

Magical uses: protection, psychic abilities, luck, employment

Shelf life: 6–9 months

SUNFLOWER OIL

Element: Fire

Gods: Apollo, Helios, Horus

Goddess: Demeter

Culinary uses: Inexpensive and good for general cooking.

Magical uses: truth, wisdom, associated with the sun, increases psychic abilities, protection

Shelf life: 9–12 months

WHEAT GERM OIL

Element: Earth

Gods: Bran, Min, Tammuz, Zeus

Goddesses: Cailleach, Ceres, Demeter, Ishtar, Isis, Onatha

Culinary uses: Good for salad dressings or as a finisher for cooked pasta. Avoid heating this oil.

Magical uses: prosperity, fertility, offering when giving thanks, protection

Shelf life: up to 4 months if stored away from light and heat

Appendix III

Correspondences by God or Goddess Name

If you are planning to work with a particular deity, you can use this list to find the rooms, elements, or festivals associated with them mentioned in this book and their food, herb, and oil correspondences.

Adammair: dill

Adonis: almond, bay leaf, corn, corn oil, fennel seed, grapeseed oil, jojoba oil, wine

Aeacus: aloe vera

Aegir: beer

Aengus mac Og: hazelnut oil

Aesculapius: bay leaf, mustard seed

Aether: Air

Agathos: rice

Aglaia: bathroom

Agni: kitchen; Fire; domestic deity; butter

Agwé: Water; anchovy

Ah-Muzen-Cab: honey

Ahti: anchovy

Áine: alfalfa

Airmid: kitchen

Albina: barley

Al-Lat: domestic deity

Amaterasu: domestic deity; lemon, soy, soybean oil

Amun-Ra: Air; aloe vera

Annapurna: domestic deity; barley

Anu (god): wine

Anu (goddess): Earth; milk

Anubis: baking soda

Aphrodite: bathroom; Water: apple, artichoke, cinnamon, honey, marjoram, olive, olive oil, oregano, rosemary, salt, sugar, thyme

Apollo: anise, apple, bay leaf, beans, olive, olive oil, orange, sunflower oil

Archemorus: parsley

Ares: black pepper, thyme

Aristaeus (The Honey Lord): cheese, honey, olive, olive oil

Artemis: almond, almond oil, aloe vera, broccoli, hazelnut oil, honey, oregano, tarragon

Arwen: apple

Asar: barley

Asclepius (Greek): canola oil, grapeseed oil, wine

Ashan: corn

Asherah: laundry room

Astara: eggs

Astarte: apple, beet, salt

Atargatis: anchovy

Athena: almond, almond oil, apple, coconut oil, olive, olive oil

Attis: almond, almond oil

Aura: Air

Auset: domestic deity (Isis)

Austeia: honey

Auxo: Earth

Axomama (Potato Mother): potato

Babalu-Aye: basil, peanut, peanut oil

Babilos: honey

Bacchus: barley, grapeseed oil, wine

Ba Chua Xu: domestic deity

Baku: child's room; domestic deity

Banana Maiden: banana

Bast: domestic deity; avocado, avocado oil, beer, cinnamon

Bat: milk

Baubo: domestic deity

Bear Goddess: garlic

Befana: onion

Belenus: Fire

Benten: domestic deity; seaweed

Benzaiten: domestic deity (Benten)

Berchta: child's bedroom; domestic deity

Bes: living room, child's bedroom; domestic deity; apple

Bibesia: grapeseed oil, wine

Blodeuwudd: Earth

Brahma: butter, eggs, olive, olive oil, tamarind

Brahmani: banana

Bran: wheat, wheat germ oil

Brighid: living room, kitchen; Fire; domestic deity; blackberry, blueberry, oats, raspberry; Imbolc

Britannia: milk

Buddha: bay leaf, mustard seed, rice

Byggvir: beer

Caelus: Air

Cailleach: wheat, wheat germ oil; Imbolc

Cardea: doorways and thresholds; domestic deity

Carnea: beans

Carya: walnut

Centeotl: corn, corn oil

Centzon Totochtin: corn, corn oil

Ceres: Earth, bay leaf, bread, corn, corn oil, oats, poppy seed, wheat, wheat germ oil

Cernunnos: bay leaf, chamomile, orange

Cerridwen: apple, bay leaf

Chandra: almond, almond oil, aloe vera

Chantico: Fire; domestic deity; chocolate

Chicomecoatl: corn, corn oil

Chieh Lin: domestic deity

Ch'uang-Kung: adult bedroom

Ch'uang-Mu: adult bedroom

Coleman Grey: domestic deity (piskies)

Corn Mother: corn, corn oil

Cupid: bay leaf, olive, olive oil, sugar

Cybele: honey

Dagda: blueberry

Daibenzaiten: domestic deity (Benten)

Daikoku: domestic deity

Daimon: rice

Damona: milk

Demeter: Earth; alfalfa, barley, bay leaf, beans, bread, honey, oats, poppy seed, rye, sunflower oil, wheat, wheat germ oil

Dewi Sri: rice

Diana: almond, almond oil, apple, broccoli, hazelnut oil, lemongrass

Dionysus: apple, barley, beer, corn, corn oil, fennel seed, grapeseed oil, wine

Djamar: salt

Doris: Water

Dugnai: bread

Durga: banana, nutmeg

Ea: honey

Ebisu: domestic deity (Daikoku)

Egres: cabbage, flaxseed, flaxseed oil

Ek Chuah: chocolate

Ellegua: allspice, basil, bergamot, cayenne, cloves, coffee, crushed red pepper, cumin, garlic, milk, peppermint, rosemary

Enki: beer

Eostre: eggs; Ostara

Epona: buckwheat

Eris: apple

Eros: bay leaf, olive, olive oil, sugar

Erzulie: tamarind

Erzulie Fréda: cardamom, peanut

Erzulie Fréda Dahomey: basil

Ethne: milk

Eurynome: Water

Fabula: beans

Fast-ta-chee: corn, corn oil

Faunus: bay leaf

Fides: bay leaf

Flora: avocado, avocado oil, broccoli, brussels sprouts, cabbage

Fornax: domestic deity; bread

Frey: apple

Freya: domestic deity; apple, rye, thyme

Gabija: Fire; domestic deity

Gaia: Earth; apple

Galatea: milk

Ganesha: domestic deity; banana, peanut, peanut oil, rice, sesame seed, sesame oil, sugar

Garbarakshambigai: castor oil

Gauri: rice

Geb: Earth

Gestin: wine

Goibniu: beer

Green Man: Earth

Gwen: apple

Gwion: corn, corn oil

Hansa: eggs

Hathor: domestic deity; avocado, avocado oil, beer, butter, coriander, eggs, grapeseed oil, milk, wine

Hebe: rosemary

Hecate: doorways and thresholds; almond, almond oil, basil, black pepper, cardamom, corn, corn oil, garlic, peppermint, sesame seed, sesame oil

Helios: cinnamon, sunflower oil

Hephaestus: Fire

Hepit: Air

Hera: Air; domestic deity; apple, milk, orange

Hercules: apple

Hermes: doorways and thresholds; almond, almond oil, anise, bay leaf, hazelnut oil, olive, olive oil

Hesat Kamadhenu: milk

Hestia: living room, kitchen; Fire; domestic deity; basil, bread

Hine-Nui-Te-Po: seaweed

Hiranyagarbha: eggs

Hobnil: chocolate

Horned God: Earth

Horus: Air; baking soda, black pepper, marjoram, onion, sunflower oil

Hou Tsi: soy, soybean oil

Hou Tu: Earth

Huitaca: raspberry

Huixtocihuatl: salt

Hulda: flaxseed, flaxseed oil

Hypnos: poppy seed

Ikatere: anchovy

Inanna: beer

Iduna: apple

Inari: rice

Indra: aloe vera, barley, olive, olive oil

Ioskeha: corn oil

Ishtar: anchovy, apple, coffee, wheat, wheat germ oil, wine

Isis: domestic deity; anchovy, barley, bread, coconut, corn, corn oil, olive, olive oil, wheat, wheat germ oil

Ithun: apple

Ivenopae: rice

Ix Chebel Yax: domestic deity

Ix U Sihnal: domestic deity (Ix Chebel Yax)

Iyatiku: corn, corn oil

Jack O'Lantern: domestic deity (piskies)

Jambhala: lemon

Janus: doorways and thresholds

Joan the Wad: domestic deities (piskies)

Juno: domestic deity; barley, peppermint

Jupiter: almond, almond oil, artichoke, broccoli, buckwheat, walnut

Kama: honey

Kamadeva: sugar

Kamadhenu: milk

Kamakshi: sugar

Kamui Fuchi: domestic deity

Kanaloa: banana

Kane: domestic deity; salt

Karpo: Earth

Kateapiairiroro: sugar

Kaya nu Hima: kitchen

Kingu: salt

Kishimo-Jin: child's bedroom, domestic deity

Knosuano: eggs

Kornjunfer: corn, corn oil

Krishna: basil, bay leaf, buckwheat, butter, milk, tamarind

Lakshmi: basil, butter, canola oil, cardamom, cumin, mustard seed, peanut

Lavangi: cloves

Lelantos: Air

Liber Pater: almond, almond oil, grapeseed oil

Lima: doorways and thresholds

Lir: Water

Lugh: apple, blackberry, blueberry, chamomile; Lammas

Luna: broccoli

Luonnotar: eggs

Mae Posop: rice

Mama Occlo: domestic deity

Mama Quilla: child's bedroom; domestic deity

Marici: Air

Mariyamman: tamarind

Mars: black pepper, coconut oil, garlic, olive, olive oil

Mary: rosemary

Maui: seaweed

Maya: sage

Mazu: Water

Mbaba Mwana Waresa: beer

Meditrina: grapeseed oil, wine

Mehet-Weret: milk

Mellonia: honey

Mercury: doorways and thresholds; almond, almond oil, anise, barley, hazelnut oil, lemongrass, olive, olive oil

Meritta: honey

Min: honey, wheat, wheat germ oil

Minerva: domestic deity; olive, olive oil

Minos: aloe vera

Minthe: peppermint, spearmint

Misor: salt

Mokosz: laundry room

Montu: black pepper

Morrigan, The: ginger

Myouonten: domestic deity (Benten)

Naavri: orange

Nana: almond

Nantosvelta: honey

Neititua Abinem: coconut

Nemesis: apple

Nephthys: baking soda

Nepit: corn, corn oil

Neptune: Water; anchovy, seaweed

Nereus: anchovy

Ninkasi: beer

Nishiki Pas: honey

Nishkende Tevtyar: honey

Nut: Air; coconut oil, milk, olive, olive oil

Obatala: almond, almond oil, cilantro, cloves, coriander, sage

Oceanus: Water

Ochun: Water; allspice, almond, almond oil, apple, apricot, apricot kernel oil, basil, chamomile, cilantro, cinnamon, coriander, cumin, hazelnut oil, honey, lemongrass, olive, olive oil, safflower oil, tamarind

Odin: almond, almond oil, apple

Oenothea: wine

Ogetsu: soy, soybean oil

Ogun: alfalfa, anise, basil, bay leaf

Oko: almond, almond oil, apricot, apricot kernel oil, black pepper, cloves, coconut oil, corn, corn oil

Olocun: Water; apple, bay leaf, cumin

Olwyn: apple

Onatha: corn, corn oil, wheat, wheat germ oil

Orion: avocado, avocado oil

Osiris: barley, beer, bread, coconut, corn, corn oil, onion

Oya: Fire; anise, cinnamon, cloves, molasses, nutmeg, star anise

Pachamama: Earth

Pamona: apple, orange

Pan: anchovy, fennel seed, honey, olive, olive oil

Pax: olive, olive oil

Pele: Fire

Pellonpekko: barley

Pemba: eggs

Perigune: asparagus, corn, corn oil

Persephone: Earth; bergamot, parsley

Pluto: peppermint, spearmint

Poludnitsa Zemyna: rye

Pontus: anchovy

Poppy Goddess: poppy seed

Poseidon: Water; anchovy, olive, olive oil, salt, seaweed

Potnia: honey

Prajapati: butter

Priapus: arugula

Prithvi: milk

Prometheus: Fire; fennel seed

Ptah: almond, almond oil

Quetzalcoatl: chocolate, corn

Ra: anchovy, bay leaf, chamomile, cinnamon, grapeseed oil, honey, olive, olive oil, wine

Radegast: beer

Raugupatis: beer

Raugutiene: beer

Rhadamanthus: aloe vera

Rhea: almond, almond oil

Rhiannon: bergamot

Rongoteus: rye

Salacia: salt

Salt Woman: salt

Saulé: laundry room; living room; Water; domestic deity; cheese, eggs, flax-seed, flaxseed oil

Sekhmet: basil, beer

Selu: corn, corn oil

Shala: barley

Shango: Air; allspice, anise, apple, apricot, apricot kernel oil, basil, bergamot, black pepper, caraway seed, cumin, ginger, molasses, safflower oil

Shesmu: grapeseed oil, wine

Shu: Air

Silenus: beer

Sri: coconut

Sulis: bathroom

Sura: grapeseed oil, wine

Surya: cinnamon

Sutr: Fire

Tages: tarragon

Tahatoi: sugar

Taliesin: barley

Tammuz: wheat, wheat germ oil

Teig: apple

Temazcalteci: bathroom

Tenenit: beer

Ten-Ten-Vilu: Earth

Te Tuna: coconut

Tezcatzontecatl: beer

Thor: hazelnut oil

Thoth: almond, almond oil

Tiamat: salt

Tjenenet: beer

Tlaloc: Water; tarragon

Tlazopilli: corn

Toyo-Uke-Bime: soy, soybean oil

Trivia: doorways and thresholds

Tulasi: basil

Ukemochi: beans, soy, soybean oil

Ukko: Air

Ukupanipo: anchovy

Usha: tamarind

Vaizgantas: flaxseed, flaxseed oil

Varuna: barley, coconut

Vedenomo: Water

Venus: bathroom; Water; alfalfa, anchovy, apple, apricot, apricot kernel oil,
    blackberry, butter, cinnamon, marjoram, rosemary, salt, sugar, tamarind

Vesta: Fire; domestic deity

Vishnu: barley, basil, bay leaf, butter, cardamom, tamarind

Vulcan: Fire; aloe vera

Wirancannos: oats

Woden: apple, chamomile

Wotan: olive, olive oil

Xilonen: corn, corn oil

Xochipilli: corn, corn oil

Xochiquetzal: chocolate

Yansa: beans

Yasigi: beer

Yellow Woman: corn, corn oil

Yemaya: Water; allspice, almond, almond oil, banana, basil, coconut oil, cumin, grapeseed oil, lemon, molasses, salt, seaweed, wine

Yum Caax: corn, corn oil

Zao Jun: living room, kitchen; domestic deity

Zeus: almond, almond oil, apple, artichoke, asparagus, bay leaf, parsley, raspberry, sage, wheat, wheat germ oil

Zosim: honey

Zytnia Matka (Rye Mother): rye

Bibliography

BOOKS

Bird, Stephanie Rose. *Sticks, Stones, Roots & Bones*. St. Paul, MN: Llewellyn: 2009.

Benhardt, Peter. *Gods and Goddesses in the Garden: Greco-Roman Mythology and the Scientific Names of Plants*. Piscataway, NJ: Rutgers University Press, 2008

Boyse, Samuel. *Heathen Gods, Heroes, Goddesses, & c.: Explain'ed in a Manner Entirely New, And Render'd Much More Useful Than Any Hitherto Publish'd on This Subject*. Dublin: J. Exshaw, 1758.

Briggs, Katharine. *An Encyclopedia of Fairies*. New York: Pantheon Books, 1976.

Budge, Sir Ernest Alfred Wallis. *The Gods of the Egyptians: Or Studies in Egyptian Mythology*. London: Methuen & Co., 1904.

Caduto, Michael J., and Rosemary Gladstar. *Everyday Herbs in Spiritual Life*. Woodstock, VT: SkyLight Paths Publishing, 2007.

Climo, Shirley, and Joyce Audy Zarins. *Piskies, Spriggans, and Other Magical Beings: Tales From the Droll-Teller*. New York: Thomas Y. Crowell, 1981.

Drew, A.J. *A Wiccan Formulary and Herbal*. Franklin Lakes, NJ: Career Press, 2004.

———. *Wicca Spellcraft for Men: A Spellbook for Male Pagans*. Franklin Lakes, NJ: Career Press, 2001.

Dunwich, Gerina. *Herbal Magick: A Witch's Guide to Herbal Folklore and Enchantments*. Franklin Lakes, NJ: Career Press, 2002.

Elias, Jason, and Katherine Ketcham. *In the House of the Moon: Reclaiming the Feminine Spirit of Healing*. New York: Hachette Book Group, 1995.

Folkard, Richard. *Plant Lore, Legend and Lyrics: Embracing the Myths, Traditions, Superstitions, and Folk-Lore of the Plant Kingdom*. London: Sampson Low, Marston, Searle, and Rivington, 1884.

Foubister, Linda. *Goddess in the Grass: Serpentine Mythology and the Great Goddess*. Victoria, BC: Ecco Nova Editions, 2003.

Gimbutas, Marija, and Miriam Robbins Dexter. *The Living Goddess*. Los Angeles: University of California Press, 2001.

Green, Aliza. *Beans*. Philadelphia: Running Press, 2004.

Hiscox, Gardner D., and Prof. T. O'Connor Sloane. *Fortunes in Formulas for Home, Farm, and Workshop: The Modern Authority for Amateur and Professional*. New York: Books, Inc., 1944.

Illes, Judika. *Encyclopedia of Spirits: The Ultimate Guide to the Magic of Fairies, Genies, Demons, Ghosts, Gods & Goddesses*. New York: HarperCollins, 2009.

Ivantis, Linda J. *Russian Folk Belief*. New York: M.E. Sharp, 1992.

Leland, Charles Godfrey. *Gypsy Sorcery and Fortune Telling: Illustrated by Incantations, Specimens of Medical Magic, Anecdotes, and Tales*. New York: University Books, 1891.

Lock, Raymond Friday. *Sweet Salt: Discovering the Sacred World of the Navajo*. Los Angeles: Mankind Pubilishing Company, 2001

Mascetti, Manuela Dunn. *Ganesha: Remover of Obstacles*. Vancouver, BC: Chronicle Books, 2000.

Monaghan, Patricia. *Encyclopedia of Goddesses and Heroines*. Santa Barbara, CA: Greenwood Press, 2010.

Murray, Michael T., Joseph Pizzorno, and Lara Pizzorno. *The Condensed Encyclopedia of Healing Foods*. New York: Simon and Schuster, 2006.

Napolitano, Peter. *Produce Pete's Farmacopeia: From Apples to Zucchini, and Everything in Between*. Lincoln, NE: Authors Choice Press: 2001.

Phillips, Henry. *History of Cultivated Vegetables; Comprising Their Botanical, Medicinal, Edible, and Chemical Qualities; Natural History; and Relation to Art, Science, and Commerce, Volume 1*. London: H. Colburn, 1822.

Pickens, Stuart D. B. *Historical Dictionary of Shinto*. Lanham, MD: Scarecrow Press, 2010.

Pughe, William Owen. *Dictionary of the Welsh Language*. West Smithfield, London: Thomas Gee, 1832.

Rajhaiah, Ratna. *How the Banana Goes to Heaven and Other Secrets of Health from the Indian Kitchen*. Daryaganj, New Delhi: Westland Ltd, 2010.

Ransome, Hilda M. *The Sacred Bee in Ancient Times and Folklore*. Mineola, NY: Courier Dover Publications, 2004.

Rogers, Mara Reid. *Onions: A Celebration of the Onion Through Recipes, Lore, and History*. Boston: Addison-Wesley Publishing Company, 1995.

Spaeth, Barbette Stanley. *The Roman Goddess Ceres*. Austin, TX: University of Texas Press, 1996.

Shurtleff, William, and Akiko Aoyagi. *History of Edamame, Green Vegetable Soybeans, and Vegetable-Type Soybeans*. Lafayette, CA: Soyinfo Center, 2009.

Stephens, Kate. *The Greek Spirit: Phases of Its Progression in Religion, Polity, Philosophy and Art*. New York: Sturgis & Walton Company, 1914.

Trinkunas, Jonas. *Of Gods & Holidays: The Baltic Heritage*. Vilnius: Tverme, 1999.

Turner, Patricia, and Charles Russell Coulter. *Dictionary of Ancient Deities*. Jefferson, NC: McFarland, 2000.

Weigle, Marta. *Spiders and Spinsters: Women and Mythology*. Santa Fe, NM: Sunstone Press, 2007.

Weiss, Peg. *Kandinsky and Old Russia: The Artist as Ethnographer and Shaman*. New Haven, CT: Yale University Press, 1995.

Williams, Charles Alfred Speed. *Chinese Symbolism and Art Motifs: An Alphabetical Compendium of Antique Legends and Beliefs, As Reflected in the Manners and Customs of the Chinese*. North Clarendon, VT: Tuttle Publishing, 1974.

Wolf, Werner. *Island of Death: A New Key to Easter Island's Culture Through an Ethno Psychological Study*. Whitefish, MT: Kessinger Publishing, 2004.

WEBSITES

Hodgson Mill. "Baking and Cooking With Flax." *www.hodgsonmill.com/tips-tricks-terms/index.php?page=baking-and-cooking-with-flax*.

Illes, Judith. "Beauty Salts." Tour Egypt. *www.touregypt.net/featurestories/salt.htm*.

Index

toys, 18, 28–29
twine, 16

U

utensils, 15

V

Vesta, 63
visions, 75

W

walnuts, 138
washers, 19
washes, 14, 75–78
Water (element), 39–42

wheat, 138–139
wheat germ oil, 179
windows, 2, 6
wine, 139
winter solstice, 146–148
wishes, 68
witch bottles, 3–5

Y

yeast, 140
Yule, 146–148

Z

Zao Jun, 63–64

About the Author

Kris Bradley started on her path to witchcraft around the age of eight, with a spiral notebook full of facts about the Roman gods and goddesses copied from an encyclopedia. When she was twelve, she received her first deck of tarot cards from her sister, and she's never looked back. Author of the popular blog *Confessions of a Pagan Soccer Mom*, Kris is also a certified Reiki practitioner/teacher and ordained minister. Her interests include tarot, gardening, the magical history of food, crafting, cooking, paranormal investigations, and various forms of energy healing. Kris lives in New Jersey with her husband, three children, a dog, and three cats.

Visit her online at *www.confessionsofapagansoccermom.com*.

To Our Readers

Weiser Books, an imprint of Red Wheel/Weiser, publishes books across the entire spectrum of occult, esoteric, speculative, and New Age subjects. Our mission is to publish quality books that will make a difference in people's lives without advocating any one particular path or field of study. We value the integrity, originality, and depth of knowledge of our authors.

Our readers are our most important resource, and we appreciate your input, suggestions, and ideas about what you would like to see published.

Visit our website at *www.redwheelweiser.com* to learn about our upcoming books and free downloads, and be sure to go to *www.redwheelweiser.com/newsletter/* to sign up for newsletters and exclusive offers.

You can also contact us at *info@redwheelweiser.com* or at

Red Wheel/Weiser, LLC
665 Third Street, Suite 400
San Francisco, CA 94107